National Certified Phlebotomy Technician Exam

"You never fail until you stop trying" - Albert Einstein

National Certified Phlebotomy Technician Exam #1

Test Taking Tips

☐ Take a deep breath and relax

☐ Read directions carefully

☐ Read the questions thoroughly

☐ Make sure you understand what is being asked

☐ Go over all of the choices before you answer

☐ Paraphrase the question

☐ Eliminate the options you know are wrong

☐ Check your work

☐ Think positively and do your best

Table of Contents

TEST DIRECTION

DIRECTIONS

Read the questions carefully and then choose the ONE best answer to each question.

Be sure to allocate your time carefully so you are able to complete the entire test within the testing session. You may go back and review your answers at any time.

You may use any available space in your test booklet for scratch work.

Questions in this booklet are not actual test questions but they are the samples for commonly asked questions.

This test aims to cover all topics which may appear on the actual test. However some topics may not be covered.

Studying this booklet will be preparing you for the actual test. It will not guarantee improving your test score but it will help you pass your exam on the first attempt.

Some useful tips for answering multiple choice questions;

- Start with the questions that you can easily answer.

- Underline the keywords in the question.

- Be sure to read all the choices given.

- Watch for keywords such as NOT, always, only, all, never, completely.

- Do not forget to answer every question.

1

Healthcare refers to the maintenance or improvement of health through prevention, diagnosis, and treatment of physical and mental illnesses.

The most common healthcare facility is **a hospital**. Hospitals are often large organizations with a complex internal structure to provide acute care to patients in need.

Which of the following services must be present in a healthcare facility to be considered as a hospital?

A) Organized medical staff
B) Therapeutic and diagnostic services
C) Permanent inpatient beds with 24-hour nursing service
D) All of the above

2

After a physician diagnoses, a patient, laboratory test, or other types of tests will come after as deemed necessary.

Which of the following consent is applicable after the patient comes to the laboratory, sleeves-rolled-up, with the physician's order?

A) Implied consent
B) Informed consent
C) Personal consent
D) Legally-binding consent

3

Which of the following terms about blood is defined correctly?

A) Apheresis is the removal of whole blood from a patient or donor.
B) Coagulation is the process by which a clot forms in the blood.
C) Blood doping is the injection of blood cells or blood substitutes to increase athletic endurance by boosting the blood stream's oxygen-carrying capacity.
D) All of the above.

CONTINUE ▶

4

Some patients in the hospital may have experienced traumatic events before being sent into the institute. The phlebotomists are expected to be caring for these types of patients.

Which of the following is to be done after a patient adamantly refuses to have his/her blood drawn?

A) Force the patient.

B) Write a note for the physician.

C) Hold the patient in place using ties.

D) Notify the physician and nurse, then wait for further instructions.

5

Which of the following prefix is not defined correctly?

A) "Hemo" means "blood."

B) "Phlebo" means "vein."

C) "Supra" means "above."

D) "Lysis" means "combine."

6

Word refers to a combination of sounds that has a meaning and is written or spoken.

Which of the following describes a suffix as an element of a word?

A) Follows the root of the word

B) Precedes the root of the word

C) Gives the definition of the word

D) Portrays the action

7

In the civilian world, the commonly used time system is the 12-hour system, where the same notation of time appears twice a day as AM and PM. This makes it easy to confuse time frames. In the military world, a slight confusion of time interpretation can be fatal. Therefore, the military improvises a time system that reduces any chances of ambiguity.

Just like in the military, health also tends to simplify time for the convenience of their operations. Differences between AM and PM are directly removed by following a 24-hour system.

Which of the following is the civilian equivalent of 1448?

A) 2:40 AM

B) 2:48 AM

C) 2:48 PM

D) 12:48 PM

8

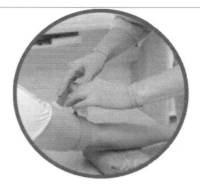

The word "**phlebotomy**", like most medical terminology, is derived from the Greek language. **Phleb** is a **prefix** meaning veins or blood vessels, and **tomy** is a suffix meaning to cut or make an incision.

What is the primary responsibility of a phlebotomist?

A) Controlling analytical variables

B) Controlling preanalytical variables

C) Controlling post-analytical variables

D) Controlling total quality management

9

The process of verifying a patient's identity and entering the information into a database is one of the duties of a phlebotomist.

Which of the following about identifying a patient and verifying the name and date of a patient's birth is correct?

A) The patient must be actively involved in the identification process.

B) You must ask the patient to state his or her full name and date of birth.

C) According to the CLSI (The Clinical & Laboratory Standards Institute) guideline GP33-A, you can ask the patient to spell the last name.

D) All of the above.

10

What is the process that involves the regulation of a specific variable in any system within the body of an organism and is defined as the overall well-being of the body?

A) Hemolysis

B) Hemostasis

C) Homeostasis

D) Hematopoiesis

11

The history of phlebotomy began with ancient cultures to treat virtually any illness. The old medical practice of phlebotomy, which was called bloodletting, is considered a pseudoscience.

Which of the following about the history of bloodletting is true?

A) Egyptians, Greeks, and Romans used bloodletting to rid the human body of evil, while the Mesopotamians and Mayans used it for ritualistic purposes.

B) In the fifth century, Greeks helped bloodletting become an actual medical procedure, allowing it to spread through other civilized areas.

C) The untimely death of the first United States president, George Washington, was thought to be excessive bloodletting. He died in 1799 after nine pints of blood were taken to treat a throat infection.

D) All of the above.

12

- Unlabeled specimens
- Improper specimen storage
- Contaminated urine specimens
- Incorrect timing of the blood draw
- Blood clots in the anticoagulated tube
- Incorrect blood volume (too little or too much)

Many factors are involved when the laboratory rejects a specimen. How many of the factors given above are the reason for specimen rejection?

A) 3

B) 4

C) 5

D) 6

13

Oxygenated blood carries enough oxygen to extend to the body tissues, providing enough oxygen to operate smoothly. Deoxygenated blood, on the other hand, is to be expelled from the body through the lungs.

Which of the following does not carry oxygenated blood?

A) Aorta

B) Radial artery

C) Pulmonary vein

D) Pulmonary artery

14

Nonverbal communication (NVC) transfers information through nonverbal platforms such as eye contact, facial expressions, gestures, and posture.

Which of the following about nonverbal communication is not correct?

A) The patient's face often tells the phlebotomist what the patient will not reveal verbally.

B) Body language, which is often conveyed unintentionally, is continuous and more reliable than verbal communication.

C) Nonverbal communication is limited, and phlebotomists can learn much about patients' feelings by verbal communication.

D) Kinesic slip is the situation when the verbal and nonverbal messages do not match. When this happens, people tend to trust what they see rather than what they hear.

A **heart disorder** is a type of condition that mainly affects the heart's functions, such as pumping the blood for blood circulation in the body. A decrease or increase in blood supply in the body may infer some heart problems if it lasts a long time.

Which of the following is a heart disorder characterized by fluid buildup in the lungs?

A) Heart attack
B) Heart stroke
C) Erratic heart beating
D) Congestive heart failure

Military Equivalent or **Military Time** is the assembly of timekeeping. The day runs from midnight to midnight and is split into 24 hours, indicated by the hours passed since midnight, from 0 to 23.

Which of the following time is the military equivalent of 11:28 AM?

A) 0128
B) 1128
C) 2328
D) 0011280

Which double membrane-bound organelle found in all eukaryotic organisms is responsible for the production of ATP where it is most abundantly found?

A) Nucleus
B) Cytoplasm
C) Mitochondria
D) Plasma Membrane

An equilibrium theoretically imposes an equivalence in the state of the body's functions. A symbiotic relationship is formed in harmony with the organs that reached a state of balance.

Which of the following is the process where the body maintains a state of equilibrium?

A) Anabolism
B) Metabolism
C) Catabolism
D) Homeostasis

19

The **pulmonary system or respiratory system** is the bodily system that enables the human body to obtain the necessary gases to work correctly. The system eliminates harmful gases, like carbon dioxide, and brings oxygen through exhaling and inhaling.

Which of the following is the purpose of the pulmonary system?

A) Carry nutrients to cells

B) Carry oxygen to and from the lungs

C) Deliver oxygen-rich blood to the brain

D) Secure the immune system by providing healthy blood cells

20

AHA: American Hospital Association
AMA: American Medical Association
CHC: Community Health Center
EHR: Electronic Health Record
PCP: Primary Care Physician
PHI: Protected Health Information
PHR: Personal Health Record
PHS: Public Health Service
PSC: Patient Service Centers

How many of the acronyms about Health Care Structure given above are correct?

A) 6

B) 7

C) 8

D) 9

21

What is the name of the cells, which are also known as white blood cells (WBCs), found in the immune system responsible for protecting the body from foreign invaders and infectious diseases?

A) Leukocyte

B) Reticulocyte

C) Erythrocyte

D) Electrolyte

22

Which of the following laboratory analyses for urologic disorders can be performed by microbiology?

A) BUN

B) PPD

C) C&S

D) FBS

23

A **blood vessel** is a passage-like vessel that carries blood throughout the body. The difference in sizes refers to their roles and where the blood is carried and originates.

Which of the following is the smallest blood vessel?

A) Vein
B) Venule
C) Capillary
D) Arteriole

24

Which of the following is not defined correctly?

A) Phlebitis is a clear fluid that separates from blood when it clots.
B) Thrombocyte is a platelet that is important for blood clotting.
C) A white blood cell is a colorless or white cell in the blood with a nucleus and cytoplasm.
D) Whole blood is the blood where none of the elements (white blood cells, red blood cells, and platelets) have been removed.

25

Latex allergy is the reaction of the immune system to specific proteins in latex rubber. Although latex allergy is rare, phlebotomists must always ask their patients about latex allergy and use latex-free equipment if they have allergies.

Which of the following are the symptoms of the latex allergy?

A) Skin redness
B) Difficulty breathing
C) Runny nose, itchy eyes
D) All of the above

26

Which of the following abbreviations is not on the Joint Commission "Do Not Use" list?

A) U
B) MP
C) IU
D) MS

CONTINUE ▶

27

Which of the following is defined as the failure to act consistently with the accepted standard of care?

A) Assault
B) Negligence
C) Malpractice
D) Dereliction

28

Healthcare is the conduct of services to patients by health professionals to prevent, diagnose, and treat disease.

Which of the following refers to the "malpractice" of healthcare?

A) Criminal action
B) Credit acquisition
C) Payment assistance
D) Professional negligence

29

The aorta is the heart's main artery that carries oxygenated blood away from the heart to flow to the rest of the body. The aortic valve prevents the backflow of blood during the pumping process.

Which of the following chambers does blood come from going to the aorta?

A) Left atrium
B) Right atrium
C) Left ventricle
D) Right ventricle

30

What is the name of the system that monitors institutions that train phlebotomists?

A) Licensure
B) Accreditation
C) Certification
D) Continuing education unit

31

Which of the following tests are defined correctly?

A) Culture and Sensitivity is a test performed to test for infections.

B) Blood culture is a laboratory test used to check for bacteria or other microorganisms in a blood sample.

C) Chemical reagent strip testing is a urine collection method that may be ordered to diagnose urinary tract infections or to evaluate the effectiveness of drug therapy.

D) All of the above

32

Which of the following laboratory tests is not helpful in the diagnosis of an HIV infection?

A) APTT

B) T-cell count

C) Western blot

D) Anti-HIV antibody

33

Which of the following is the meaning of the prefix anti-?

A) For

B) Among

C) Against

D) Between

34

Whole blood is the human blood from a standard blood donation.

Which of the following are not found in whole blood?

A) Casts

B) Platelets

C) Erythrocytes

D) Lymphocytes

CONTINUE ▶

35

When venipuncture cannot be performed, a dermal puncture may be required. A dermal puncture may be a fingerstick or maybe a heel stick in the case of small infants.

Which of the following statements is true when performing a dermal puncture?

A) The puncture must be aligned with the whorls of the fingerprint.

B) The puncture must be perpendicular to the whorls of the fingerprint.

C) The puncture must be on the edge of the finger.

D) The puncture must be on the tip of the finger.

36

The heart is an essential organ of the body that manages the blood's pumping in the body. The heartbeats indicate the work of the heart to keep the blood circulation in the body.

Which of the following is the thick muscle layer of the heart?

A) Myocardium

B) Endocardium

C) Epicardium

D) Pericardium

37

A **chain of custody** is the detailed documentation showing the experiment's sequential procedure done in a sample, which includes the collection, analysis, storage, and disposal of the sample.

Which of the following kinds of consequences requires a chain of custody for a specimen?

A) Legal

B) Adverse

C) Infectious

D) All samples need a chain of custody.

38

Which one of the following organizations prepares the guidelines and principles of laboratory practices to assure the quality and integrity of phlebotomy?

A) PHS: Public Health Service

B) ACA: American Certification Agency

C) CLSI: The Clinical and Laboratory Standards Institute

D) HCFA: Health Care Financing Administration

CONTINUE ▶

39

Medical negligence can be proven in many ways. It is commonly proven to provide evidence for medical malpractice.

Which of the following is not an example of medical negligence?

A) The phlebotomist does not put the needle in a proper container.
B) The phlebotomist does not return the bed to the previous position.
C) The phlebotomist fails to obtain a specimen from a combative patient.
D) The phlebotomist reports a different result which can lead to complications.

40

Bleeding or **blood loss** refers to blood escaping from the body due to damaged blood vessels. This phenomenon may be due to medical conditions, injuries, or a combination of both.

How long does it take for the body to replace 500 mL of blood?

A) 2-4 weeks
B) 6-8 weeks
C) 10-12 weeks
D) 12-14 weeks

41

The **DNA** of a patient is contained in the cells present in his/her body. The hair, nails, and saliva can contain DNA.

Which of the following part of a cell contains the chromosomes or genetic material?

A) Nucleus
B) Cytoplasm
C) Cell membrane
D) Golgi Apparatus

42

A laboratory test must be conducted with the recommendation of a healthcare professional. The results are deemed confidential and can only be viewed as information to aid the patient's medical condition.

Which of the following is required for the patient's result to be legally released in public?

A) Provide written consent
B) Express permission through a video feed
C) Allow his/her lawyer to release it according to his/her preference.
D) All of the above

CONTINUE ▶

43

Gases in the body can be found mostly in the blood flowing in the blood vessels. It is easier to spot the gases near the lungs or the smaller blood vessels.

Which of the following is the site where most gas exchange between blood and tissue takes place?

A) Venules

B) Arterioles

C) Capillaries

D) Pulmonary vein

44

Which of the abbreviations about the laboratory is correct?

A) LIS: Laboratory information system

B) MLS: Medical Laboratory Scientist

C) GLPs: Good laboratory practices

D) All of the above

45

Which of the following does the abbreviation "NPO" mean?

A) New protocol only

B) Nothing by mouth

C) No precipitation occurs

D) Negative platelet outcome

46

A medical term is a specifically used word for medical practice. These words are used to explain, define, and point different medical knowledge.

Which of the following defines the structure and determines the meaning of a medical term?

A) Suffix first, prefix next, and root word last.

B) Prefix first, suffix next, and root word last.

C) Root word first, prefix next, and suffix last.

D) Root word first, suffix next, and prefix last.

47

Which of the following about the blood is correct?

A) Hemolysis is the destruction of red blood cells.
B) Hematoma is the collection of blood underneath the skin, also known as a bruise.
C) Hemoconcentration is the excessive accumulation of blood into an area of the body, usually caused by a tourniquet left on too long or a patient pumping their fist.
D) All of the above

48

Which of the abbreviations about blood is correct?

A) BAC: Blood alcohol concentration
B) BBP: Bloodborne pathogen
C) ACT: Activated clotting time
D) All of the above

49

Verbal communication refers to the use of language or words to express ideas.

Which of the following is true when you communicate verbally with a patient?

A) Use nonmedical terms so patients can understand
B) Never give false reassurance to patients such as, "It won't hurt."
C) Explain the procedures to gain the confidence and cooperation of the patients
D) All of the above

50

Which of the following terms refers to the volume percentage of packed red blood cells in a blood sample?

A) Hematuria
B) Hematoma
C) Hematocrit
D) Hemoglobin

51

Which of the following about the immune system is defined correctly?

A) An antibody is a type of protein the immune system produces to neutralize a threat of some kind.

B) An antigen is any substance capable of inducing a specific immune response and triggering an antibody's production specific to that substance.

C) Immunocompromised is the impairment of the immune response, usually due to disease, medication therapy, or surgery.

D) All of the above

52

Which of the following are the responsibilities of the Bureau of the Fiscal Service or commonly known as Fiscal Services, which is an agency of the United States federal government?

A) Performing tests

B) Cleaning and maintenance

C) Diagnosis and treatment of the patient

D) Admitting, medical records, and billing

53

The main goal of a phlebotomist is to assist the healthcare team in the accurate, reliable, and safe collection and transportation of specimens for testing.

Which of the following actions is the legal responsibility of a phlebotomist while doing his job?

A) Follow the standard of care.

B) Maintain patient confidentiality.

C) Maintain the integrity of the doctor-patient relationship.

D) All of the above.

54

TSH is a hormone that activates the pituitary gland, resulting in the production of thyroxine and triiodothyronine.

In phlebotomy, TSH stands for which of the following terms?

A) Thyroid Specific Hormone

B) Thyroid Sufficient Hormone

C) Thyroid Stimulating Hormone

D) None of the above

CONTINUE ▶

55

Which of the phlebotomy terms given below is defined correctly?

A) Accession is the process of recording in the order it was received.

B) The form which is used to enter the test orders is called a requisition.

C) The behavior of a healthcare provider toward a patient is called bedside manner.

D) All of the above.

56

A requisition is a formal order to obtain and use a document or other materials. The requisition of data in a hospital can provide the relevant details of the request or order.

Which of the following is required in the patient's requisition of information?

A) Patient's full name

B) Ordering physician's name

C) Type of test to be performed

D) All of the above

57

A bleeding time test is a medical test done on someone to assess his/her platelet function. During the test, a patient is made bleed then the time it takes to stop bleeding is measured.

Which of the following medication does not interfere with the bleeding time test?

A) Aspirin

B) Ethanol

C) Ibuprofen

D) Acetaminophen

58

The blood specimens obtained by a phlebotomist can be differentiated in how they are received, the container in which they are contained, and the additives added right away. The phlebotomist knows which kind of specimen can be collected from the patient.

Which of the following is the significant difference between plasma and serum?

A) Plasma looks clear; the serum is cloudy.

B) Plasma looks cloudy, the serum is not

C) Plasma contains fibrinogen; the serum does not

D) Plasma contains minerals; the serum does not

59

Which of the following prefixes does thromb- refer to?

A) Tumor
B) Clotting
C) Hemolysis
D) Lymphostasis

60

A **telephone protocol** is the standard way of answering a telephone call. The receiver is usually the one providing the protocol to the caller.

Which of the following is not a proper telephone protocol?

A) Hang up on angry callers
B) Answer the phone properly
C) Make the callers a priority, if necessary
D) Clarify and record information of the caller

CONTINUE ▶

61

Phlebotomists are given voluntary permission to touch a patient for blood collection. Some patients may question the appropriateness of touching because it can convey many different meanings based on their cultural background.

Which of the following explanation about touching is not correct?

A) Phlebotomist's touching to the patient is a kind of social touching.

B) Therapeutic touch (TT) can be used by a phlebotomist to reduce the anxiety of the patient.

C) Patients are much more aware of phlebotomist's touch than phlebotomist is of theirs.

D) It is a particular type of nonverbal communication to provide caring and ensure comfort.

62

Which of the following is the meaning of the suffix -tomy?

A) To cut

B) Study of

C) Opening

D) Shape or form

63

Minor refers to the classification of people in terms of age, support, and responsibility.

Which of the following applies to the real definition of a minor?

A) Has parental responsibility

B) Living under parent's house

C) Younger than 18 years of age

D) Has not reached the age of majority

64

Which of the following is the principal defense against a malpractice suit?

A) Denying liability

B) Showing a burden of proof

C) Reaching an out-of-court settlement

D) Showing that the standard of care was followed

CONTINUE ▶

65

Which department is responsible for studying the diagnosis, cause, treatment, and prevention of blood-related diseases, mostly responsible for conducting complete blood count (CBC)?

A) Serology department
B) Urinalysis department
C) Chemistry department
D) Hematology department

66

Which of the following is the duty of a phlebotomist?

A) Providing patients with containers for the collection of random samples.
B) Always confirming with the patients that they have understood the instructions.
C) Providing instructions to the health-care provider's office personnel when it is requested.
D) All of the above.

67

A typical newborn will have around 10% of blood in proportion to his weight. 100mL of blood is usually measured for every kilogram.

Which of the following is the blood volume of an infant weighing 6 lbs?

A) 245 mL
B) 270 mL
C) 700 mL
D) 1.7 mL

68

The **lymph** is a Latin word for "water." The lymph is the fluid that flows through the lymphatic system made up of lymphatic vessels and nodes.

Which of the following does lymph originate from?

A) Serum
B) Plasma
C) Joint fluid
D) Tissue fluid

69

In phlebotomy, the abbreviation PP stands for which of the following terms?

A) Post-Prandial
B) Post Procedure
C) Post-Partutition
D) Platelet Procedure

70

Plasma and serum are two elements of blood. **Plasma** makes up about 55% of the overall blood volume, and **serum** is plasma minus the clotting factors and blood cells.

Which of the following is not right about the serum and plasma?

A) Plasma contains fibrinogen, but serum does not.
B) Plasma is mostly used for blood-clotting-related problems.
C) Serum is mostly used for blood typing but is also used for diagnostic testing.
D) Plasma is obtained after the clotting of blood, while serum is derived before the blood's coagulation.

71

The atrium is the top chamber of the heart. Which of the following is the plural form of atrium?

A) Atria
B) Atrial
C) Atrium
D) Atriume

72

Which of the following departments is also allowed to draw arterial blood gases aside from the laboratory?

A) Radiology department
B) Physical therapy department
C) Respiratory therapy department
D) Occupational therapy department

73

Which of the following agencies is handling all disaster situations?

A) NIH
B) FEMA
C) JCAHO
D) The Governor's Office

74

If a phlebotomist ignores the refusal or forcibly tries to collect a sample from a patient who refuses to have blood drawn, which of the following charges can he/she be accused of?

A) Libel
B) Slander
C) Assault and battery
D) Invasion of privacy

75

Lab abbreviation refers to a short form of a laboratory word or phrase used to shorten the terms for easy understanding.

Which of the following lab abbreviations defines the laboratory word "PT"?

A) Part Time
B) Pregnancy Test
C) Prothrombin Time
D) Partial thromboplastin

76

What is the functional unit of the nervous system that is an electrically excitable cell that transmits and processes information using electrical and chemical signals?

A) Nephron
B) Neuron
C) Neoplasm
D) Nucleus

77

What is the chemistry department section usually associated with drug analysis since they are concerned with studying the detection, nature, and adverse effects of different chemicals on living organisms?

A) Cardiology

B) Toxicology

C) Immunology

D) Electrophoresis

78

Unopette system is a method for diluting blood when preparing for counting blood cells.

Which of the following tests can use the Unopette system?

A) Chemistry

B) Coagulation

C) Hematology

D) Blood banking

79

Which of the following is a medical field that involves the use of radioisotopes to perform tests for the diagnosis and treatment of diseases?

A) Hematology

B) Cytogenetics

C) Nuclear medicine

D) Respiratory therapy

80

HIPAA, or the Health Insurance Portability and Accountability Act of 1996, is an act in the United States that protects the confidentiality of a patient's medical details and other data that identifies the patient.

Under this Act, which of the following elements is not necessarily considered a piece of protected health information?

A) Patient's full name

B) Patient's employment records

C) Patient's medical record numbers

D) Patient's date of discharge from hospital

Deoxygenated blood is the blood that already finished supplying oxygen to the body. It has run out of oxygen to distribute, so it has to exit the stream while obtaining more oxygen and releasing carbon dioxide.

Which of the following chambers does the deoxygenated blood enter?

A) Left atrium

B) Right atrium

C) Left ventricle

D) Right ventricle

A patient has the right to refuse medication and the tests prescribed by his/her healthcare professional. Although it is not common, some healthcare professionals require the patient to sign a waiver to refuse the treatment or test.

Which of the following cases will most probably let the patient feel in control?

A) Insist that the patient let you draw blood

B) Require the patient to be cooperative without question

C) Let the patient know that his/her doctor requires him/her to provide blood

D) Agree with the patient that it is his right to refuse to have a blood specimen drawn

83

Which of the following must they consult, if phlebotomists want to compare previous patient data with current patient data?

A) Delta check
B) Collection logbook
C) Accession numbers
D) Postanalytical variables

84

Which of the following kinds of information can be disclosed according to the patients' rights?

A) Only those information related to health care
B) All health-related information
C) As little information as needed
D) Adequate amounts of the most recent information

85

Which of the following **common blood disorders** is defined correctly?

A) Hemochromatosis: High iron count, iron overload
B) Sickle cell disease: Abnormal hemoglobin, inherited red blood cell disorder
C) Polycythemia vera: High red blood cell count, the bone marrow makes too many red blood cells
D) All of the above

86

The blood flow in the human body systematically follows a set pattern. Backflow is guaranteed not to happen as long as the valves are working correctly.

Which of the following are listed in the proper order of blood flow?

A) Capillary, venule, vein
B) Vein, venule, capillary
C) Venule, vein, capillary
D) Vein, capillary, venule

87

What part of the circulatory system does the exchange of gas occur and is considered the smallest type of blood vessel that is only one cell layer thick?

A) Capillaries
B) Veins
C) Arteries
D) Venules

CONTINUE ▶

Anticoagulants, commonly known as **blood thinners,** are medicines that help prevent blood clots. They work by interrupting the process involved in forming blood clots and decreasing the blood's ability to clot. They're sometimes called "blood-thinning" medicines, although they don't actually make the blood thinner.

Which of the following is right about anticoagulants?

A) The most common side effect of treatment with anticoagulant medicine is bleeding.
B) Anticoagulants such as heparin or warfarin (also called Coumadin) slow down your body's process of making clots.
C) They're given to people at a high risk of getting clots to reduce their chances of developing severe conditions such as strokes and heart attacks.
D) All of the above.

89

A body organ is a part of the body that has a particular purpose or function.

Which of the following body organs is mainly affected in a person with a pulmonary disease?

A) Brain
B) Heart
C) Lungs
D) Neck

The walls of the blood vessels protect it from bursting and sudden puncture. The thickness of the walls will help develop a clot whenever a blood flow outside the system is detected.

Which of the following is the type of muscle found on the walls of blood vessels?

A) Neural
B) Skeletal
C) Visceral
D) Pulmonary

91

Valves are the blood vessels' gate-like apparatus that acts to prevent a backward flow of blood. It keeps blood circulation in the body by blocking the unneeded backflow from other blood vessels.

Which of the following does not have a valve?

A) Capillaries
B) Left ventricle
C) Right ventricle
D) Saphenous vein

92

Dermal puncture is an alternative to venipuncture to obtain the blood sample.

Which test is collected first during a dermal puncture?

A) Electrolytes
B) Blood smear
C) Platelet counts
D) Complete blood count (CBC)

93

The **bleeding time (BT)** is the time between making a small incision and the moment when the bleeding stops. It may be longer in children and tends to take slightly longer in females than in males.

Which of the following time intervals is the typical result for an average bleeding time?

A) 30 to 45 seconds
B) 2 to 10 minutes
C) 10 to 20 minutes
D) 15 to 20 minutes

94

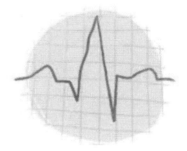

An electrocardiogram (ECG) is a test that uses electrical pulses from the heart to determine problems relating to the organ.

Which of the following causes the P waves in an ECG?

A) Atrial contractions
B) Delayed contractions
C) Advanced contractions
D) Differential contractions

95

Solutions are commonly used in laboratories for testing and research. These solutions can be concentrated or diluted according to the needs of the medical staff.

Which of the following can produce a 1:10 solution of bleach?

A) 1 mL bleach to 99 mL water

B) 1 mL water to 9 mL bleach

C) 10 mL bleach to 90 mL water

D) 10 mL water to 90 mL bleach

96

Capillary blood is obtained by pricking a finger in adults and a heel in infants and small children.

Which finger is commonly used and preferred for capillary collection?

A) Pinky

B) Thumb

C) Ring finger

D) Index finger

97

A **specimen** refers to a sample to be tested like blood or body tissue for medical purposes. On the other hand, **the serum** is a protein-rich liquid used to separate the blood when it coagulates.

Norma is scheduled for a blood test. The procedure indicates that the volume ratio for the serum to the specimen is 1:1. The test requires 3mL of serum. The laboratory, then, requires that the amount of blood to be collected should be 250% of the needed specimen's volume.

Which of the following tube sizes should be used to collect the specimen?

A) 5 mL

B) 8 mL

C) 10 mL

D) 15 mL

98

Gerry, a phlebotomist, has a patient who refuses to have blood drawn from him.

Which of the following actions should he take?

A) He should notify a family member.

B) He should ensure that he notifies the patient's doctor promptly.

C) He should persuade the patient to comply with the drawing of blood.

D) He should perform the phlebotomy regardless of whether the patient allows them to or not.

99

In human anatomy, some terms with specific anatomical meanings are used to talk about the locations of bones and their features.

Which of the following terms are explained correctly?

A) Superior: Higher, Inferior: Lower

B) Anterior: Toward the front, Posterior: Toward the rear.

C) Medial: Toward the middle, close to the center of the body, Lateral: Toward the side, away from the center of the body

D) All of the above

100

A phlebotomist ignores a patient who refuses a procedure and continues to prepare for the process.

Which of the following can the phlebotomist be accused of?

A) Assault

B) Battery

C) Defamation

D) Breach of Confidentiality

101

A typical adult has an average blood volume of 70 mL per kilogram. The blood volume varies depending on many aspects like diet and family history.

Which of the following is an average man's blood volume if he weighs 130 lbs?

A) 3.5 L

B) 4.7 L

C) 4.1 L

D) 5.2 L

102

The creation of new blood cells that are needed by the body from hematopoietic stem cells is called **hematopoiesis**. Hematopoietic stem cells eventually specialize or differentiate into myeloid cells.

In which organ system does the hematopoiesis occur?

A) Skeletal system

B) Nervous system

C) Muscular system

D) Digestive system

103

The heel of the foot is the most preferred site for dermal puncture and capillary blood collection.

How many mm/cm is the maximum depth of a heel puncture?

A) 3.0 mm

B) 2.0 mm

C) 2.0 cm

D) 1.5 cm

104

Which of the following is a blood test that is usually handled by the coagulation department that measures the time the blood takes to clot and check if medicine used to prevent blood clots work?

A) Electrolytes

B) Bacterial growth

C) Prothrombin times

D) Complete blood counts

105

Heel stick is a simple procedure in which a newborn baby's heel is pricked, and then a small amount of the blood is collected, usually with a narrow-gauge glass tube or a filter paper. It is an accessible way and minimally invasive of obtaining capillary blood samples that can be used for succeeding lab tests.

Where are heel sticks usually located?

A) At the arch

B) At the posterior surface

C) At the center of the plantar surface

D) At the lateral or medial borders of the plantar surface

106

A condition that occurs when digestive enzymes become activated while still in the pancreas causing inflammation is called **pancreatitis**.

Which of the following laboratory tests should be performed to screen pancreatitis?

A) CSF

B) Myoglobin

C) Occult blood

D) Serum amylase

107

Plasma is the transparent liquid portion of blood that remains after all the other blood components are removed. It consists of water, salts, enzymes, antibodies, and other proteins.

What percent of the total blood volume is constituted by plasma?

A) 80%

B) 92%

C) 55%

D) 45%

108

Which of the following leukocytes protects the body by ingesting or phagocytosing harmful foreign particles such as dead cells and bacteria?

A) Basophils

B) Neutrophils

C) Eosinophils

D) Lymphocytes

109

Helper T cells are the most critical cells in adaptive immunity since they are required for almost all adaptive immune responses.

Which of the following are produced with the help of Helper T cells?

A) Antigens

B) Cytokines

C) Antibodies

D) Interleukins

110

A **tort** is a term in common law jurisdictions defined as a wrongful act that causes suffering to another person, which eventually results in legal liability.

Where does a tort originate?

A) Public law

B) Civil action

C) Criminal action

D) Out-of-court settlement

111

What is the allowed maximum elapsed time between the time a sample is collected and the time the plasma or serum is separated from the formed elements?

A) 30 minutes

B) 1 hour

C) 2 hours

D) 3 hours

112

What type of tissue supports, connects, binds, or separates organs and other tissues from each other?

A) Nerve tissue

B) Muscle tissue

C) Epithelial tissue

D) Connective tissue

SECTION 1 BASICS OF PHLEBOTOMY

#	Answer	Topic	Subtopic	#	Answer	Topic	Subtopic	#	Answer	Topic	Subtopic	#	Answer	Topic	Subtopic
1	D	TA	S1	29	C	TA	S2	57	B	TA	S4	85	D	TA	S2
2	B	TA	S5	30	B	TA	S2	58	C	TA	S2	86	A	TA	S2
3	D	TA	S2	31	D	TA	S4	59	B	TA	S4	87	A	TA	S2
4	D	TA	S3	32	A	TA	S2	60	A	TA	S5	88	D	TA	S4
5	D	TA	S4	33	C	TA	S4	61	A	TA	S3	89	C	TA	S4
6	A	TA	S4	34	A	TA	S3	62	A	TA	S4	90	C	TA	S2
7	C	TA	S4	35	B	TA	S4	63	D	TA	S5	91	A	TA	S2
8	B	TA	S3	36	A	TA	S2	64	D	TA	S2	92	B	TA	S4
9	D	TA	S1	37	A	TA	S5	65	D	TA	S1	93	B	TA	S4
10	C	TA	S2	38	C	TA	S4	66	D	TA	S3	94	A	TA	S2
11	D	TA	S3	39	C	TA	S5	67	B	TA	S4	95	C	TA	S4
12	D	TA	S1	40	B	TA	S2	68	D	TA	S2	96	C	TA	S4
13	D	TA	S2	41	A	TA	S2	69	A	TA	S4	97	D	TA	S4
14	C	TA	S3	42	A	TA	S5	70	D	TA	S2	98	B	TA	S2
15	D	TA	S2	43	C	TA	S2	71	A	TA	S4	99	D	TA	S2
16	B	TA	S4	44	D	TA	S4	72	C	TA	S1	100	A	TA	S5
17	C	TA	S2	45	B	TA	S4	73	B	TA	S5	101	C	TA	S4
18	D	TA	S2	46	A	TA	S4	74	C	TA	S5	102	A	TA	S2
19	B	TA	S2	47	D	TA	S2	75	C	TA	S4	103	B	TA	S4
20	D	TA	S1	48	D	TA	S4	76	B	TA	S2	104	C	TA	S1
21	A	TA	S2	49	D	TA	S3	77	B	TA	S1	105	D	TA	S4
22	C	TA	S2	50	C	TA	S4	78	C	TA	S4	106	D	TA	S2
23	C	TA	S2	51	D	TA	S2	79	C	TA	S1	107	C	TA	S2
24	A	TA	S4	52	D	TA	S1	80	B	TA	S5	108	B	TA	S2
25	D	TA	S3	53	D	TA	S2	81	B	TA	S2	109	C	TA	S2
26	B	TA	S4	54	C	TA	S4	82	D	TA	S5	110	B	TA	S2
27	B	TA	S2	55	D	TA	S3	83	A	TA	S2	111	C	TA	S2
28	D	TA	S5	56	D	TA	S3	84	B	TA	S5	112	D	TA	S2

Topics & Subtopics

Code	Description	Code	Description
SA1	Health Care Structure	SA4	Medical Terminology
SA2	Human Anatomy & Physiology	SA5	Legal & Ethics
SA3	Introduction to Phlebotomy	TA	Basics of Phlebotomy

CONTINUE ▶

TEST DIRECTION

DIRECTIONS

Read the questions carefully and then choose the ONE best answer to each question.

Be sure to allocate your time carefully so you are able to complete the entire test within the testing session. You may go back and review your answers at any time.

You may use any available space in your test booklet for scratch work.

Questions in this booklet are not actual test questions but they are the samples for commonly asked questions.

This test aims to cover all topics which may appear on the actual test. However some topics may not be covered.

Studying this booklet will be preparing you for the actual test. It will not guarantee improving your test score but it will help you pass your exam on the first attempt.

Some useful tips for answering multiple choice questions;

- Start with the questions that you can easily answer.

- Underline the keywords in the question.

- Be sure to read all the choices given.

- Watch for keywords such as NOT, always, only, all, never, completely.

- Do not forget to answer every question.

1

Among the following diseases, which one requires the patients to be given therapeutic phlebotomies?

A) Hemochromatosis

B) Leukemia

C) Polycythemia

D) A and C

3

Safety and security must be emphasized when using medical apparatus that may possibly harm the user if misused. Tools that have high voltage must be used with proper caution and expertise.

Which of the following must not be done when a person receives an electrical shock?

A) Turn off the circuit breaker.

B) Move the electrical source using wood.

C) Move the electrical source using a glass object.

D) Pull the person away from the electrical source.

2

A phlebotomist must undergo training and education in a certified institute before taking the exam. Laboratory and clinical classes are the places where gloves must be worn for infection control.

Which of the following should a student do if he/she found rashes on the skin after wearing gloves in the first training week?

A) Do not use gloves

B) Inform the instructor

C) Use a different brand of gloves

D) Take anti-allergenic medicine to remove the rash

CONTINUE ▶

4

Hemolysis refers to the disruption of the red blood cells, leading to the release of hemoglobin.

In a laboratory setup, which of the following actions can lead to a blood specimen's hemolysis?

A) Retracting a syringe plunger with light pressure.
B) Inserting a needle into the alcohol-air-dried site.
C) Using a 21-gauge needle to fill up a 10-mL red-stoppered tube.
D) Combining the blood with an additive or anticoagulant through shaking.

5

Which of the following refers to the order of draw?

A) It is the order in which tubes are filled.
B) It is a sequence wherein you store blood vials.
C) It is the sequence in which you choose patients to draw blood from.
D) It is an order made by the supervisor to collect blood from a patient.

6

Chloe is collecting a blood sample from a patient in Room 17. However, her patient was beginning to feel faint in the middle of blood collection.

Which of the following actions must Chloe take?

A) Stop the blood draw so that the patient will have time to recover.
B) Ask for assistance and wait until it comes to proceed to blood collection.
C) Pull out the needle, advise the patient to lower his/her head, and report the issue.
D) Tell the patient to relax and take deep breaths until the end of the blood collection.

7

Which of the following terms about infection is defined correctly?

A) Infection is the invasion and proliferation of pathogens in body tissues.
B) Fomite is any nonliving object or substance that is capable of carrying infectious organisms.
C) Protozoon is a single-cell parasite that replicates rapidly once inside a living host.
D) All of the above

CONTINUE ▶

8

Which of the following tests gives valuable results regarding whether a patient has experienced a myocardial infarction?

A) Glucose
B) Cholesterol
C) Hemoglobin
D) Cardiac troponin T (cTnT)

9

When a phlebotomist performs an eosinophil count, which of the following blood parts is being measured?

A) Platelets
B) Red blood cells
C) White blood cells
D) All of the above

10

Alcohols are the most commonly used disinfectants in the medical field. They are volatile chemicals used to sterilize patients' skin before skin puncture or surgery and disinfect the hands of healthcare professionals.

In which of the following situations is the use of alcohol-based hand rub not allowed?

A) Before eating
B) After touching the patient
C) Before touching the patient
D) After throwing out uncontaminated gloves

11

Which of the following characteristics does not affect blood composition?

A) Age
B) Gender
C) Altitude
D) Weight

12

Which of the following fluids is not considered as a stat specimen?

A) Urine
B) Synovial fluid
C) Peritoneal fluid
D) Cerebrospinal fluid

13

Inert materials such as clothes, furniture, and utensils can also transmit infectious substances from one person to another.

In phlebotomy, which of the following refers to these objects?

A) Germs
B) Fomites
C) Parasites
D) None of the above

14

Which of the following specimens must be chilled first when transferring it to the laboratory?

A) Ammonia
B) Cryoglobin
C) Cryofibrinogen
D) Cold agglutinins

15

An arterial blood sample is collected from an artery, primarily to determine arterial blood gases. The sample can be obtained through a catheter placed in an artery or a needle and syringe to puncture an artery.

How long do you have to wait after injecting lidocaine before the anesthetic effects in arterial blood collection?

A) 1 to 2 minutes
B) 2 to 3 minutes
C) 3 to 4 minutes
D) 4 to 5 minutes

CONTINUE ▶

An **isolation room** is created for the sake of keeping a patient from outside contact. It is only available upon the recommendation of the healthcare worker in-charge, like a doctor or specialist.

Which of the following is the PPE that must be removed outside the room upon exit of the isolation chamber?

A) Gown

B) Gloves

C) Face mask

D) Respirator

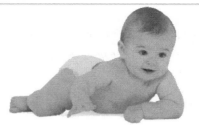

Which of the following statements is true regarding newborns or infants?

A) Newborns and infants are prone to infection.

B) More blood is required from newborns to provide plasma or serum for testing.

C) Newborns have a more significant amount of plasma compared with adults.

D) Newborns have a more significant amount of red blood cells compared with adults.

18

The **blood pressure** measured by a device is the pressure present on the blood vessels' walls caused by the circulating blood.

Which of the following is the systolic pressure obtained from?

A) Cuff has been fully deflated.

B) An artery has been compressed, and blood flow is cut off.

C) Muffled sound that is heard as the cuff deflates

D) First heart sounds that is heard as the cuff deflates

19

Collecting blood samples from infants is more challenging as compared to blood collection from adults.

As a phlebotomist, which of the following measures is a proper blood sampling procedure at the neonatal intensive care unit?

A) Wear a lab coat, mask, and gloves

B) Do not wake the infant up to draw blood properly

C) Clean the skin puncture site using povidone-iodine

D) Place the blood drawing tray as closer to the isolette as possible.

20

The Occupational Safety and Health Administration, or OSHA, requires the healthcare worker's employers to provide the necessary equipment and materials that they may need for personal safety and health.

Which of the following is not required to be provided to the employees?

A) Protection equipment

B) Hepatitis B Vaccine (HBV) immunization

C) Hepatitis C Vaccine (HCV) immunization

D) Human Immunodeficiency Virus (HIV) immunization

A **tourniquet** is a medical device commonly used for venipuncture. The device is designed to help the phlebotomist collect blood more efficiently.

Which of the following is the primary use of a tourniquet?

A) Concentrate the blood specimen
B) Help find and enter the veins easily
C) Keep the vein healthy during the process.
D) All of the above

A **tourniquet** refers to a medical tool that aims to lessen the blood flow on the patient's limb or other body parts to allow faster blood clotting in an exterior wound.

Which of the following is the timeframe needed when using a tourniquet on a patient?

A) At most 1 minute
B) At least 3 minutes
C) Approximately 4 minutes
D) Until it is told to do so by a medical practitioner

23

The **order of draw** is a recommended order of the drawing of blood for the specimens to be used on the patient's tests.

Which of the following is the order of draw if a CBC, PT, plasma potassium and glucose (with glycolysis inhibitor) should be collected during a multiple-tube draw on a patient?

A) Purple, light blue, gold, green

B) Light blue, green, lavender, gray

C) Light green, orange, lavender, gray

D) Orange, royal blue, green, lavender

24

Which of the following is defined correctly?

A) Bevel is a sharpened and slanted cut edge of a needle designed to ease the process of puncturing tissue.

B) The catheter is a hollow, flexible tube inserted into a vessel or cavity of the body to withdraw fluids.

C) Aerobic blood culture bottle is the type of blood culture bottle used to collect specimens to test for microbes that thrive in the air.

D) All of the above

25

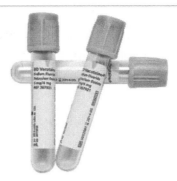

What would most likely happen when a stopper is removed from a blood collection tube?

A) Clotting

B) Aerosol

C) Glycolysis

D) Hemolysis

26

Most specimens are used in a laboratory test within an hour or two. This is to ensure that the microorganisms that need to be detected live are still present.

Which of the following is the specimen that needs to be chilled before a test?

A) Bilirubin

B) Blood glucose

C) Complete blood count

D) None of the above

CONTINUE ▶

27

During the collection of timed specimens, what factor is being monitored?

A) Bilirubin
B) Medication levels
C) Cold agglutinins
D) Cryoglobulins

28

A **throat culture** is a type of laboratory test that focuses on the diagnosis of fungi or harmful bacteria present in the throat. The sample is obtained through cotton that is swabbed in the throat.

Which of the following is the area that can be used to collect a throat culture sample?

A) Lips
B) Teeth
C) Gums
D) Tonsils

29

The laboratory has the right to refuse certain specimens. Which of the following is not a reason for specimen rejection?

A) A CBC collected in a lithium heparin tube
B) An EDTA tubes used for a chemistry test
C) A sodium level collected in a sodium heparin tube
D) A cold agglutinin sample transported in a heel warmer

30

The body clots the blood through the skin opening to prevent it from flowing out more than necessary. The body cannot close the wound through clotting in a short time if it is more extensive.

Which of the following tubes will have the blood contained to clot within 5 minutes?

A) RST
B) PST
C) SSP
D) PST

31

Jaundice is a term used to describe a yellowish tinge to the skin and the eye's whites.

If a patient has jaundice, which of the following biological components must be tested?

A) Glucose

B) Bilirubin

C) Electrolytes

D) Complete blood count (CBC)

32

At room temperature, how long does it take for blood clotting to complete?

A) 10 to 15 minutes

B) 20 to 30 minutes

C) 30 to 45 minutes

D) 1 hour

33

Coumadin, generically known as **warfarin**, is a medicine used to thin out the body's blood by acting as an anticoagulant. The chemical can be lethal if taken with proper supervision from a physician.

Which of the following tests monitors a Coumadin Therapy?

A) ACT

B) APTT

C) CuHcg

D) None of the above

34

What condition typically occurs as a person grows older?

A) The layers of the skin tend to become more elastic.

B) Hematomas are more likely to occur.

C) Arteries move further away from the surface of the skin.

D) Blood vessels widen due to atherosclerosis.

CONTINUE ▶

35

Which of the following safety equipment may be included in the lab to ensure the safety of anyone who is working there?

A) Eyewash station

B) Emergency shower

C) Personal protective equipment

D) All of the above

36

What are the two pretesting conditions that must be met before performing the dipstick test for routine urinalysis?

A) The sample must be at room temperature and well mixed.

B) The sample must be refrigerated and centrifuged.

C) The sample must be warmed to body temperature and mixed well.

D) The sample must be at room temperature and centrifuged.

37

Medical personnel follows several guidelines for isolation precautions to prevent the spread of infectious microorganisms.

According to the recent CDC isolation guidelines, which of the following are the three new sets of isolation and disease-specific precautions?

A) Airborne, droplet, and contact

B) Droplet, complete, and airborne

C) Enteric, contact, and respiratory

D) Contact, airborne, and respiratory

38

When working with supplies other than sharps in a laboratory, which of the following options is the correct way of garbage and used supplies disposal?

A) Throw directly in the trash.

B) Put in puncture-resistant containers.

C) Place in labeled biohazard containers.

D) Place them in double garbage bags and throw them in the trash.

Jaundice has many causes, including hepatitis, gallstones, and tumors. It happens when too much bilirubin (a chemical released by the red blood cells during their normal breakdown process) builds up in the blood.

Which of the following is observed when a person has jaundice?

A) Swelling of the skin

B) Bruising of the skin

C) Yellowing of the skin

D) None of the above

A urine test can be required by a physician to determine immediate chemicals or elements in the patient's metabolic system. The presence of these chemicals may confirm the details of your illness or disorder.

Which of the following tests requires a patient to collect a midstream clean-catch sample?

A) Drug test

B) Pregnancy test

C) Alcohol volume test

D) Culture and sensitivity test

Reverse isolation is the kind of isolation used to prevent germs from invading your body when your immune system fails or is not working well. Germs can be carried on most items like clothes and through air and water droplets.

In which of the following cases can reverse isolation be used?

A) A patient with AIDS

B) A patient with measles

C) A patient with severe burns

D) A patient with lung infection

A healthcare worker must be conscious of preventing the spread of disease to the environment. Before leaving the hospital, it is recommended to apply disinfectant and clean properly to avoid bringing germs and viruses with you.

Which of the following is the most important mean of preventing the spread of infection?

A) Wearing gown

B) Wearing mask

C) Wearing gloves

D) Proper hand antisepsis

CONTINUE ▶

43

Blood-borne pathogens are pathogens that spread through blood contact or intake. Some of these pathogens only require the victim to be splashed with a small amount of blood to be transferred to the new host.

Which of the following examples of potential exposure to blood-borne pathogens involves a parenteral route of transmission?

A) Eating chips while experimenting

B) Rubbing the eyes while processing specimens

C) Sucking fingers while reading a laboratory manual

D) Chewing gum while collecting blood specimen

44

Phlebotomists perform their routine blood collections early in the morning.

Which of the following explains why the blood is collected early in the morning?

A) The laboratory needs the results early.

B) Patients have a lower chance of fainting syndrome.

C) The blood pressures of the patients are not high in the mornings.

D) Patients are in a basal state, approximately 12 hours after the last ingestion of food or other nutrition.

45

What factor is not assigned to a sample that is subject to laboratory tests?

A) Sample type

B) Accession number

C) Name of the collector of the sample

D) Name of the person depositing the sample in the lab

46

When collecting an 8-hour specimen, which time of the day is it typically collected?

A) After a meal

B) In the morning

C) Before going to bed

D) Any time during the day

A good quality check ensures that a test goes well. The test will have almost 100% success due to a well-done quality check.

Which of the following is ensured with a good quality check?

A) Correct patient identification

B) Correct performance of the test

C) The integrity of testing materials

D) Correct functioning of the testing apparatus

A fasting glucose test requires the patient to fast for at least 8 hours before the blood specimen can be collected. The patient can drink water, but no food can be taken before specimen collection.

Which of the following should be done when the patient is in the act of eating before you can collect the specimen?

A) Collect the blood while the patient is eating.

B) Stop the patient and then collect the blood.

C) Fill out the form and add a note that the patient ate before collection.

D) Consult with the patient's nurse to verify if the specimen should be collected.

Engineering controls are the procedures built into designing a plant, method, or apparatus to minimize the hazard.

Which of the following options is an example of engineering control that eradicates threats posed by bloodborne pathogens?

A) Gloves

B) Sharps container

C) Laboratory gown

D) Universal precautions statement

Safety in the hospital can be divided into many levels, like electrical safety, equipment safety, radiation safety, and others. Since the hospital is a complex environment, the healthcare worker should be mindful of what kind of protection must be applied in the area that he/she may interact with.

Which of the following do the distance, time, and shielding principles belong?

A) PPE safety

B) Water safety

C) Radiation safety

D) Personal safety

Micro-collection is a procedure wherein a small puncture is made in the skin to access the capillary bed.

For this process, which of the following is the best way to increase blood flow?

A) Warming up the site

B) Applying a tourniquet

C) Applying firm pressure to the site

D) Starting two successive punctures

Which of the following urine test is the most widely used to determine pregnancy?

A) Timed urine

B) Fasting urine

C) Random urine

D) First morning urine

53

What factor is being tested when a 72-hour stool specimen is collected?

A) Fat quantities

B) Occult blood

C) Creatine levels

D) Protein concentrations

54

Needlestick injuries usually happen when healthcare professionals, especially phlebotomists, accidentally puncture their skin whenever they use, dispose of, or disassemble needles.

Which of the following measures is an excellent way to avoid needlestick injuries?

A) Putting back needle caps by hand.

B) Waiting until the needle trash container is full before emptying it.

C) Utilizing safe needle tools and following directions for proper usage and disposal.

D) Turning the safe needle device on just before putting it in the sharps disposal container.

Although the hospitals seem to be competing in their expertise, a globally recognized threat, like epidemics and widespread viruses, everyone is required to contribute to their capabilities to ensure that the overall population's safety is not threatened to a severe level.

Which of the following is signified by a globally harmonized signal word?

A) Chemical invention

B) Newly discovered element

C) The severity of a hazard faced

D) Type of hazard that is introduced globally

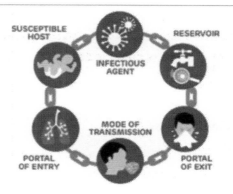

The **chain of infection** is not an actual chain but an imaginary chain formed by linking different unique points of infection. Each of the links can be broken or interrupted through various means.

Where does the susceptible host live and multiply in this chain?

A) Reservoir

B) Portal of exit

C) Portal of hosting

D) Transmission means

Which of the following is not a complication during arterial blood gas (ABG) collection?

A) Petechiae
B) Hematoma
C) Thrombosis
D) Arteriospasm

How many seconds/minutes should the heel of a newborn be warmed for a dermal puncture?

A) 30 seconds
B) 1 to 2 minutes
C) 3 to 5 minutes
D) 6 to 8 minutes

Anticoagulants are used in testing the blood of a patient and prevent it from clotting. EDTA, sodium citrate, and potassium oxalate are the anticoagulants used in blood collection tubes.

Which of the following does an anticoagulant do to prevent blood clotting?

A) Binding calcium
B) Releasing pheromones
C) Binding the fibrous cells
D) Acting as an anti-thrombin agent

The yellow substance that is excreted by the body when replacing old red blood cells is called bilirubin.

Which of the following statements is correct about the transport of infant bilirubin?

A) Infant bilirubin must be transported on ice.
B) Infant bilirubin must be transported in amber-colored microtubes.
C) Infant bilirubin must be transported in a heel warmer.
D) There are no special transport measures necessary.

CONTINUE ▶

61

Phlebotomy procedure is not performed when an arm contains which of the following?

A) A fistula
B) An arterial line
C) A heparin lock
D) An implanted port

62

Phlebotomy refers to the act of collecting or removing blood from the body through a puncture or an incision for blood analysis. The technique is done to diagnose a possible disease or for the treatment of a patient.

Which of the following actions must never be done when performing a phlebotomy procedure?

A) Recap all needles.
B) Reach for the falling needle.
C) Put down an unsheathed needle.
D) All of the above

63

Which of the following should you do first when giving breathing aid to a victim?

A) Clear the airway.
B) Begin mouth-to-mouth ventilation.
C) Place the victim on a firm, flat surface.
D) Determine whether the victim is conscious or not.

64

Colored blood collection tubes indicate which types of blood specimen they must be filled with. The tube colors can also display the ratio of additives added to the blood inside the tube.

Which of the following stopper-colored tubes must be filled in an exact ratio?

A) Red stopper
B) Green stopper
C) Light green stopper
D) Light blue stopper

Airborne precautions are necessary to shield individuals, especially vulnerable ones, against infectious diseases' airborne transmission.

Isolation is used when a patient has a suspected or confirmed case of which disease?

A) Measles

B) Influenza

C) Gangrene

D) Hepatitis A

Personal protective equipment (PPE) helps prevent the spread of germs in the hospital. This can protect hospital staff, patients, visitors, and health care workers from infections. PPE is used by the hospital staff when there is contact with blood or other bodily fluids.

Which of the following is not included in PPE?

A) Masks

B) Gloves

C) Uniforms

D) Apron or gown

Bone marrow refers to the sponge-like tissue that is present in most of your bones. The marrow is inside the bone, which contains stem cells that mainly develops into red blood cells.

From which of the following bones should a bone marrow sample be collected?

A) Femur

B) Radius

C) Iliac crest

D) Hip bones

Which of the following terms refers to an individual who has recovered from a specific virus and has established antibodies against that particular microbe?

A) Carrier

B) Immune

C) Infectious

D) Vulnerable

69

Newborn babies must undergo neonatal screening to determine different illnesses that may develop as they grow older. A hearing test and other various tests are also given to ensure that the baby does not have other disabilities.

Which of the following is the baby's required age to undergo a blood spot testing for neonatal disorder screening?

A) 12 hours old
B) 18 hours old
C) 36 hours old
D) 72 hours old

70

Infection refers to the incursion and propagation of microorganisms, such as viruses and bacteria that are not ordinarily present in the body. It can lead to mild or severe diseases, depending on the degree of microorganism invasion.

Which of the following descriptions refers to an indirect infection?

A) It is transmitted through kissing.
B) It is transmitted through direct contact.
C) It is transmitted through sexual intercourse.
D) It is transmitted through no direct human contact.

71

Which of the following specimen is used during blood culture collection?

A) A chilled specimen
B) A peak and trough specimen
C) Aerobic and anaerobic specimen
D) An accompanying urine specimen

72

Different laboratory tests require various media and the collection of specimens. Blood tests have other varieties that involve different tools to obtain a result.

Which of the following laboratory tests is photosensitive?

A) Glucose test that measures the amount of glucose in your blood
B) Complete blood typing, which is a method to tell what type of blood you have
C) Hematocrit blood testing, which is performed to determine the number of red blood cells in a person's blood
D) None of the above

CONTINUE ▶

73

Immunosuppression is a reduction of the activation of the immune system. Some portions of the immune system may have immunosuppressive effects on other parts of the immune system.

Why is it so essential to place highly immunosuppressed patients in a protective environment?

A) It prevents transmission of infection to the patient.
B) It protects the general public from disease.
C) It prevents the transmission of infection from the patient.
D) It protects the patient from spores in the environment.

74

Phlebotomists need great caution when handling different blood samples to avoid contamination of the collected specimen and prevent them from being infected with unwanted agents.

Which of the following is the most effective method in preventing the proliferation of infection?

A) Always use clean gloves.
B) Apply proper hand hygiene.
C) Put on a protective face mask.
D) Always wear personal protective equipment.

75

The site for capillary puncture is usually located in the earlobe, fingers, or heels. The phlebotomist can choose which part to collect and draw blood, but it is easier to collect from the fingers.

Which of the following conditions disqualifies a site for a capillary puncture?

A) Swollen
B) Cyanotic
C) Edematous
D) All of the above

76

Which of the following compounds is not light sensitive?

A) Bilirubin
B) Lactic acid
C) Vitamin A
D) Beta-carotene

77

Skin puncture is done on infants to draw enough blood since their veins and capillaries are tiny. It is not recommended to use a needle to obtain a small amount of blood from a newborn infant.

Which of the following is the specimen collected first when a skin puncture is performed on an infant?

A) Hematology
B) Immunology
C) Blood banking
D) Blood chemistry

78

What is preferred by phlebotomists to use when performing dermal punctures in pediatric patients?

A) PKU testing
B) Serum testing
C) Crossmatch testing
D) Blood culture testing

79

Laboratory healthcare workers are usually at risk of being infected with the samples they are handling. These workers must ensure that they are wearing complete PPE to maintain this risk at a minimum.

Which of the following is the most frequently occurring lab-acquired infection?

A) AIDS
B) Hepatitis B
C) Dengue Fever
D) Skin infection

80

Which of the following is defined correctly?

A) Osmosis is the diffusion of water through a semipermeable membrane.
B) The diluent is a solution (such as water or saline) that reduces a specimen's concentration.
C) Diffusion is the movement of a substance from an area of high concentration to low concentration.
D) All of the above

81

POCT refers to the extensive testing conducted outside a clinical laboratory. It is usually performed by non-laboratory personnel and close to where a patient is given care.

Which of the following terms corresponds to the abbreviation POCT?

A) Point of Care Testing
B) Point of Contact Testing
C) Pre-Occupational Care Testing
D) None of the above

82

Before and after medical procedures, the healthcare worker must maintain cleanliness, like applying rubbing alcohol to the hands. Disinfectants effectively control the spread of bacteria and viruses, which are usually transmitted through physical interaction.

Which of the following is the recommended disinfectant for blood and body fluid contamination?

A) Sodium benzoate
B) Sulfuric solution
C) Hydrogen peroxide
D) Sodium hypochlorite

83

Newborn screening is conducted to detect and determine the newborn's possible defects upon birth.

Which of the following is a part of newborn screening tests wherein blood is collected using filter paper?

A) PKU
B) CBC
C) Bilirubin
D) Electrolytes

84

A blood sample tube is an apparatus used to collect and store the blood of a patient. A tube will have different indications like colors or markers to let the practitioner know how much and which part the blood should be drawn.

Which of the following tubes must be filled first while collecting blood samples?

A) Red
B) Green
C) Purple
D) Blood culture

85

A **HemoCue Analyzer** is an advanced device used for quantitative diagnostic determination of the blood's hemoglobin levels. The device includes a specially designed photometer, analyzer, and cuvettes.

Which of the following will indicate that a patient has anemia using a waived test via a HemoCue Analyzer?

A) Glucose
B) Bilirubin
C) Monotest
D) Electrolytes

86

What is incorporated to ensure a successful Point-Of-Care Testing (POCT) program?

A) Adherence to the manufacturer's instructions
B) Use of quality-assurance and quality-control procedures
C) Proper and adequate training of all personnel
D) All of the above

87

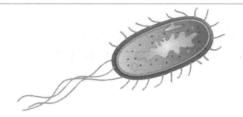

Which part of the body has several types of Escherichia coli as its normal flora?

A) Colon
B) Urinary tract
C) Respiratory tract
D) Circulatory system

88

A **biocide** is a general term used to refer to chemicals that destructively kill the biological organism.

Which of the following is a biocide?

A) Povidone-iodine
B) Hydrogen peroxide
C) 70% isopropyl alcohol
D) All of the above

89

HO

OH

HO

H
N

When performing an epinephrine tolerance test, which of the following is being determined?

A) The patient's ability to mobilized glycogen from the liver
B) The patient's ability to digest lactose
C) The patient's ability to metabolize carbohydrates
D) The patient's ability to metabolize medications

90

A two-hour postprandial test is used to determine the blood glucose levels after a meal.

Which of the following is being tested by a two-hour postprandial test?

A) Malaria
B) Diabetes mellitus
C) Medication levels
D) Blood alcohol levels

91

A lancet can refer to different tools in medicine. A blood lancet is used for pricking or puncturing the superficial capillary near the skin.

Which of the following is the deepest puncture allowed for a blood lancet, according to CLSI?

A) 1.0 mm
B) 1.5 mm
C) 2.0 mm
D) 3.0 mm

92

Which of the following machine is misdescribed?

A) The cholestech is used for testing cholesterol and related lipids.
B) A statSpin is a type of machine used to separate the serum or plasma from blood cells.
C) A scarpel is a surgical tool used in many surgical procedures to control bleeding.
D) A glucometer is a home measurement system you can use to test the amount of glucose in your blood.

CONTINUE ▶

93

Which of the following is the most effective way to stop the spread of infection?

A) PPE
B) Hand hygiene
C) Isolation procedures
D) Standard precautions

94

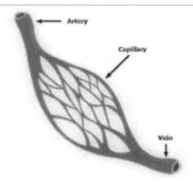

A **capillary** in the human body is a blood vessel branching from the bigger arteries. These capillaries supply the blood to the smaller parts of the body that does not need too much blood flow.

Which of the following is the main reason for a capillary draw?

A) Veins are fragile
B) Patient is overweight
C) Small amount of blood is needed
D) The capillary capacity is ordered to be studied

An **arterial blood gas test** is a technique used to measure the amount of oxygen and carbon dioxide in the blood. The analysis shows the lungs' efficiency in moving the arterial gases in and out of the body.

If a blood sample is subjected to an arterial blood gas test, the analysis must be performed within how many minutes after sample collection?

A) 15 minutes
B) 30 minutes
C) 45 minutes
D) 60 minutes

Which of the following procedure should be followed when making smears for malaria?

A) Prepare two regular smears only.
B) Prepare two to three regular smears and one thick smear.
C) Prepare one thick smear only.
D) Prepare one regular smear and one thick smear.

The heart is subdivided into four main chambers. The atrium and ventricles are divided into two sides, namely left and right.

Which of the following chambers receives oxygenated blood from pulmonary circulation?

A) Left atrium
B) Right atrium
C) Left ventricle
D) Right ventricle

The feces of a patient may contain information that can be the cause of the illness or disorder. A fecal analysis requires a sample obtained depending on the test that the patient will have to undergo.

Which of the following would require a patient to collect a 72-hour fecal sample?

A) Fecal fat analysis
B) Fecal occult blood
C) Fecal ova and parasites
D) Fecal culture and sensitivity

99

What is the size of the needle gauge that is typically used to collect blood that will be subjected to an ABG test?

A) 16 gauge
B) 20 gauge
C) 22 gauge
D) 18 gauge

100

In phlebotomy, which of the following is considered the more dangerous act when considering the patient's well-being?

A) Improper disposal of sharp objects.
B) Needle recapping after performing venipuncture.
C) Putting labels on collection tubes before blood gathering.
D) Not wearing safety gloves during the venipuncture procedure.

101

What test is used to diagnose whooping cough, croup, and pneumonia, which usually do not require a physician for specimen collection?

A) SE tests
B) Urinalysis
C) NP culture
D) Throat swap

102

Which of the following actions can minimize the damage of red blood cells or hemolysis?

A) Prewarming the sample
B) Vigorous mixing of the specimen
C) Immediate separation of cells from the plasma or serum
D) Ensuring specimen tubes are always upright

103

CDC or Centers for Disease Control and Prevention developed infection control policies to help hospitals and healthcare workers prevent disease spread. These policies are regulated and changed based on studies and research.

Which of the following is the CDC-made routine infection control policy followed in all healthcare settings?

A) Universal precautions
B) Standard precautions
C) Unilateral precautions
D) Healthcare precautions

104

$$WBC \rangle \frac{Hgb}{HCT} \langle PLT$$

Capillary puncture offers a less invasive procedure for the patient. The patient will also experience lesser pain as compared to a venous puncture.

Which of the following is collected first using a capillary puncture?

A) CBC
B) Glucose
C) Electrolytes
D) Calcium ascorbate

105

The chain of infection helps gather the details needed to prevent the spread of infection.

Which of the following is the correct order of continuous links in the chain of infection?

A) Means of transmission, susceptible host, source
B) Source, means of transmission, susceptible host
C) Susceptible host, source, means of transmission
D) None of the above.

106

A **pathogen** is a microorganism or a biological agent that can cause illness or disease to its host and is usually used for disrupting the normal physiology of multicellular organisms.

Which of the following is not classified as a pathogen?

A) Fungi
B) Viruses
C) Vectors
D) Bacteria

107

Which of the following protective equipment has to be worn first and taken off last when wearing and taking off personal protective equipment?

A) Mask
B) Gown
C) Gloves
D) Shoe covers

108

The analysis used to detect infection-causing germs such as fungi or bacteria and determine what kind of medicines will work best to treat the illness or infection is called the **culture & sensitivity test** or **C&S test**.

Among the samples given, which one is not used for C&S?

A) Random samples
B) Clean catch samples
C) Suprapubic samples
D) Catheterized samples

109

The NFPA diamond is composed of four smaller diamonds with different colors, indicating specific hazard information.

What does the yellow diamond in the NFPA label indicate?

A) Flammability
B) Health hazards
C) Specific Hazards
D) Reactivity warning

110

When performing a venipuncture, which vein should be the priority since it is relatively close to the arm's surface and becomes more visible when pressure is applied to it?

A) Iliac vein
B) Basilic vein
C) Median vein
D) Cephalic vein

111

The arterial blood gas (ABG) test is used to measure the acidity of the blood using pH and the carbon dioxide and oxygen levels found in the blood collected from an artery.

Which of the following is used to coat a syringe used to draw blood for an ABG test?

A) EDTA
B) Heparin
C) Sodium citrate
D) Sodium fluoride

112

The agency responsible for regulating all work environments preventing any accidents by providing standards and guidelines for accident prevention is the Occupational Safety and Health Administration (OSHA).

Among the precautions given below, which does not belong to OSHA standard?

A) All biohazard material must be labeled.

B) Employees must practice standard precautions.

C) Employers must have written airborne pathogen exposure control plans in the workplace.

D) Employers must provide immunization against hepatitis B virus free of charge.

SECTION 2 PROCEDURES

#	Answer	Topic	Subtopic	#	Answer	Topic	Subtopic	#	Answer	Topic	Subtopic	#	Answer	Topic	Subtopic
1	D	TB	S2	29	B	TB	S4	57	A	TB	S2	85	C	TB	S2
2	B	TB	S3	30	A	TB	S2	58	C	TB	S2	86	D	TB	S1
3	D	TB	S1	31	B	TB	S2	59	A	TB	S4	87	A	TB	S3
4	D	TB	S4	32	C	TB	S4	60	B	TB	S4	88	D	TB	S2
5	A	TB	S2	33	B	TB	S2	61	A	TB	S2	89	A	TB	S2
6	C	TB	S1	34	B	TB	S2	62	D	TB	S1	90	B	TB	S2
7	D	TB	S3	35	D	TB	S1	63	D	TB	S1	91	C	TB	S1
8	D	TB	S1	36	A	TB	S1	64	D	TB	S2	92	C	TB	S1
9	C	TB	S4	37	A	TB	S3	65	A	TB	S3	93	B	TB	S3
10	A	TB	S1	38	C	TB	S3	66	C	TB	S3	94	A	TB	S2
11	D	TB	S2	39	C	TB	S2	67	C	TB	S2	95	A	TB	S4
12	A	TB	S2	40	D	TB	S2	68	B	TB	S3	96	B	TB	S2
13	B	TB	S3	41	C	TB	S3	69	D	TB	S2	97	A	TB	S2
14	A	TB	S2	42	D	TB	S3	70	D	TB	S3	98	A	TB	S2
15	A	TB	S2	43	B	TB	S3	71	C	TB	S2	99	C	TB	S2
16	D	TB	S3	44	D	TB	S2	72	D	TB	S4	100	C	TB	S1
17	C	TB	S2	45	B	TB	S4	73	A	TB	S3	101	C	TB	S2
18	D	TB	S2	46	B	TB	S2	74	B	TB	S3	102	C	TB	S4
19	A	TB	S3	47	C	TB	S2	75	D	TB	S2	103	B	TB	S3
20	C	TB	S3	48	D	TB	S2	76	B	TB	S2	104	A	TB	S2
21	B	TB	S2	49	B	TB	S3	77	A	TB	S2	105	B	TB	S3
22	A	TB	S2	50	C	TB	S3	78	A	TB	S2	106	C	TB	S3
23	B	TB	S2	51	A	TB	S2	79	B	TB	S3	107	B	TB	S3
24	D	TB	S2	52	D	TB	S2	80	D	TB	S4	108	A	TB	S2
25	B	TB	S4	53	A	TB	S2	81	A	TB	S1	109	D	TB	S1
26	D	TB	S4	54	C	TB	S1	82	D	TB	S3	110	C	TB	S1
27	B	TB	S2	55	C	TB	S3	83	C	TB	S2	111	B	TB	S2
28	D	TB	S2	56	A	TB	S3	84	D	TB	S2	112	C	TB	S3

Topics & Subtopics

Code	Description	Code	Description
SB1	Care & Safety	SB4	Specimen Transport Handling & Processing
SB2	Collection Procedures	TB	Procedures
SB3	Infection Control		

CONTINUE ▶

TEST DIRECTION

DIRECTIONS

Read the questions carefully and then choose the ONE best answer to each question.

Be sure to allocate your time carefully so you are able to complete the entire test within the testing session. You may go back and review your answers at any time.

You may use any available space in your test booklet for scratch work.

Questions in this booklet are not actual test questions but they are the samples for commonly asked questions.

This test aims to cover all topics which may appear on the actual test. However some topics may not be covered.

Studying this booklet will be preparing you for the actual test. It will not guarantee improving your test score but it will help you pass your exam on the first attempt.

Some useful tips for answering multiple choice questions;

- Start with the questions that you can easily answer.

- Underline the keywords in the question.

- Be sure to read all the choices given.

- Watch for keywords such as NOT, always, only, all, never, completely.

- Do not forget to answer every question.

1

Although blood specimens may seem the same to the patient's view, collecting a blood specimen requires different procedures depending on the test(s) it may undergo.

Which of the following test cannot be completed by a blood specimen obtained from a capillary puncture?

A) PTT

B) Hgb

C) Lead

D) Bilirubin

2

Thanks to medical advances, the self-sealing septums automatically seal themselves after the needle's insertion to transfer liquid or medicine.

Which of the following has a self-sealing septum that is accessed with a non-coring needle?

A) PICC line

B) Hickman tube

C) Implanted port

D) Bilateral IV

3

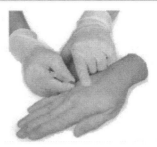

A hand venipuncture is suitable for children because of the smaller veins on their elbows. The phlebotomist will have a better procedure in a hand venipuncture for small children.

Where is the tourniquet applied when doing a hand venipuncture?

A) Distal to the wrist bone

B) Proximal to the wrist bone

C) Proximal to the elbow bones

D) A tourniquet is not required

4

Fiona was assigned to collect blood samples from one patient for blood culture, complete blood count, and lactic acid testing.

Which of the following specimens can she collect by skin puncture?

A) Samples for blood culture and lactic acid testing only.

B) Samples for blood culture and complete blood count only.

C) Samples for lactic acid testing and total blood count only.

D) All samples can be collected using skin puncture.

5

Blood collection tubes are usually marked with different colors. Hospitals use this marking to determine what test the blood specimen will be used for.

Which of the following is the time the phlebotomist labels the blood collection tube?

A) Before blood collection

B) After the specimen has been collected

C) After the assigned nurse verifies the specimen

D) After the physician signs the blood collection tube

6

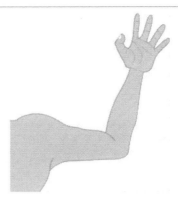

The **elbow pit** is the most common site for blood collection in phlebotomy. This area contains the antecubital veins, which are much visible compared to other veins in the body; hence, they are an excellent blood collection site.

Which of the following antecubital veins is the last option to draw blood?

A) Basilic vein

B) Brachial vein

C) Cephalic vein

D) Median cubital vein

69

CONTINUE ▶

7

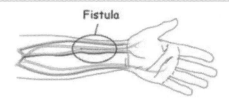

Fistula

A **fistula** is an unusual connection between tissues or blood vessels. It also applies to other body parts caused by infection or surgery.

Which of the following must a phlebotomist do if she encounters a fistula on the patient's arm?

A) Use the other arm
B) Apply the tourniquet above the fistula
C) Apply the tourniquet below the fistula
D) Draw the blood on the vein without a fistula

8

Nia has been analyzing blood samples for the presence of small amounts of metals.

Which of the following color-stoppered tubes should she use for this type of analysis?

A) Green
B) Orange
C) Dark blue
D) Red (plastic)

9

A **dermal puncture** is a back-up solution upon failure of doing a venipuncture. Fragile or small veins are the usual causes for being unable to perform the procedure.

Which of the following is the most critical condition for selecting a dermal puncture device?

A) Required tests
B) Depth of incision
C) Width of incision
D) Length of incision

10

There may be different reasons for blood to stop flowing during venipuncture.

Which of the following are the suggested actions if blood stops flowing during the blood collection?

A) Apply heat or gently massage above the vein if there is a venous spasm.
B) Release the tourniquet, allow the vein to refill, and reapply the tourniquet if it is a collapsed vein.
C) Draw the needle back if the needle is inserted too far, remove it immediately and apply pressure if there is bruising.
D) All of the above

11

Most seniors sent to the hospital have illnesses caused by their weak immune systems or failing organs. Blood drawing for these patients can be difficult as they are becoming delicate with age.

Which of the following is a proper procedure when dealing with an elderly patient?

A) Ask the elderly to be cooperative without asking consent.

B) Speak loudly to be sure that you will not repeat what you have said.

C) Make sure to hold adequate pressure after the draw until bleeding stops.

D) Inform the attendant about the procedure and let them talk to the patient.

12

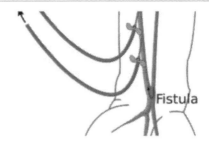

An **arteriovenous fistula** is an unusual connection between a vein and an artery. It might be artificially introduced, but it can also be acquired through a pathological process.

Which of the following patients is most likely to have an arteriovenous fistula?

A) Cancer

B) Dialysis

C) Alzheimer's

D) Regular Outpatient

CONTINUE ▶

13

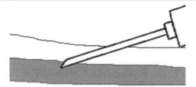

When performing a venipuncture, the entry angle must be carefully studied and approximated for the procedure to proceed appropriately. The excessive increase in angle may hurt the patient or tear the vein causing internal bleeding.

Which of the following is the recommended angle of needle insertion when performing venipuncture on an arm vein and a hand vein, respectively?

A) 20 degrees or less, 10 degrees or less

B) 30 degrees or less, 20 degrees or less

C) 30 degrees or less, 10 degrees or less

D) 45 degrees or less, 20 degrees or less

14

Blood culture bottles are used for blood culture tests, which determine the presence of bacteria or microorganisms in your blood. A blood infection may be declared if any of these are found in significant amounts.

What should be done first when blood is inoculated into blood culture bottles while using a winged blood collection set?

A) Inoculate aerobic bottle

B) Activate safety equipment

C) Inoculate anaerobic bottle

D) Decrease the volume of inoculated blood

CONTINUE ▶

15

The phlebotomist must ensure that the site of venipuncture will be able to hold the needle in place. Some veins are too fragile to be able to handle the extraction process.

Which of the following is the preferred vein for venipuncture in the "H" pattern?

A) Basilic vein

B) Cephalic vein

C) Median cubital

D) Superficial cephalic vein

16

Choosing a good site for the venipuncture procedure will lessen the risk of introducing complications to the patient.

Which of the following can qualify as an area for venipuncture?

A) Tattoos

B) Hematomas

C) Edematous tissues

D) Deep cephalic veins

17

A **butterfly needle** is a hollow needle that has plastic "wings" on the side. It is used to access the veins and is commonly used in venipuncture. After inserting the butterfly needle, the phlebotomist must seat the needle.

Which of the following explains the meaning of seating the needle?

A) Keep the skin dry during the procedure.

B) Slightly thread it within the lumen of the vein.

C) Let the patient hold it personally after the insertion.

D) Push the bevel against the back wall of the vein.

18

Grace, a phlebotomy technician, is working on a blood analysis that involves reversible anticoagulant citrate.

Which of the following color-stoppered tubes should she use?

A) Pink

B) Grey

C) Black

D) Light blue

Minor bruising is the most common reaction to venipuncture. Although severe risks are relatively rare, some conditions can trigger serious venipuncture complications.

Which of the following condition that can cause venipuncture reaction is not defined correctly?

A) Diaphoresis is the perspiring from sweat glands, often a response to stress, exercise, or heat.

B) Phlebitis is the inflammation of the vein. It can occur due to blood clot(s) in a vein that causes inflammation.

C) Syncope is a sudden, uncontrolled electrical disturbance in the brain that can alter a patient's behavior, movements, or feelings.

D) Cellulitis is a common but potentially serious bacterial infection of the skin. The affected areas typically appear swollen and red.

Bruising, also called a **contusion,** is caused by bleeding under the skin, which may occur due to injury to blood vessels during the practice of drawing blood from a vein.

Which of the following is true about the treatment of bruises?

A) Applying cold compresses to the bruised area can help to relieve any pain or discomfort.

B) The patient must be warned to avoid lifting heavy objects for a few days since it can aggravate the bruising.

C) The patient must be warned that bruises usually fade away in about 2 weeks. If the bruise isn't improving after 2 weeks patient must be warned to talk to a doctor.

D) All of the above.

An **ESR test** is a blood test that assesses the speed of the red blood cells to sink at the bottom of a test tube that contains a blood specimen.

Which of the following tubes should be used when performing an ESR test?

A) Red
B) Black
C) Lavender
D) Light yellow

A **hematoma**, a collection of blood outside of a blood vessel, can result from an injury to any blood vessel. Phlebotomy procedures can also cause a hematoma.

Which of the following does not cause hematoma?

A) Excessive anchoring of the needle to the vein
B) Late removal of the tourniquet after the blood draw
C) Asking the patient to bend the elbow and apply pressure
D) Bandaging the patient's arm immediately after needle removal

Phlebotomists use different colors of tube stoppers on tube samples to distinguish the contents of each tube.

Which of the following tube stopper colors does not suggest the presence (or absence) and the kind of additive contained in the tube?

A) Green
B) Lavender
C) Light blue
D) Royal blue

The venipuncture site must be well-defined as it is crucial to have a durable vein for the procedure. The patient must also indicate any discomfort to the phlebotomist to ensure that the process does not introduce any complications.

Which of the following is right for a paralyzed arm?

A) It has a lot of hematomas.
B) It has no sensory damage.
C) It has no muscle functions.
D) It is a permanent condition.

25

A breathalyzer is medical laboratory equipment to determine blood alcohol levels.

Which of the following can cause a falsely decreased blood alcohol level in the lab?

A) The tube is fully filled.
B) The tube is partially filled.
C) Blood is collected in a gray stopper tube.
D) The site is cleaned with Zephiran chloride.

26

Sometimes, a venipuncture procedure can be very complicated, depending on the patient's situation. It is easier to persuade and explain to an adult as compared to a child who thinks that needles are scary.

Which of the following is the best approach to use on an 8-year old child who needs to have blood drawn?

A) Have someone restrain the child and collect the specimen.
B) Bribe the child with some candy to carry on with the procedure.
C) Ask the child to be cooperative to be released sooner from the hospital.
D) Explain the blood drawing in simple terms and ask for the child's cooperation.

27

Arterial puncture is the same procedure as venipuncture but is aimed at the arteries near the wrist. The blood specimen collected is usually used for an ABG test.

Which of the following complications are associated with arterial puncture?

A) Infection
B) Hematoma
C) Arteriopasm
D) All of the above

28

An **arteriovenous fistula** is an unusual or abnormal connection between the vein and an artery. The connection may be artificially introduced or caused by an illness or accident.

Which of the following does an AV fistula commonly used for?

A) Venipuncture
B) Dialysis access
C) Blood infusion
D) Chemotherapy

## 29

Usually, a capillary puncture is conducted for children and infants that do not have sturdy and larger veins for venipuncture. The capillary puncture is also used if the patient is fragile, in general.

Which of the following is the reason for performing a capillary puncture on adults?

A) Veins are only for chemotherapy

B) The patient has thrombotic tendencies.

C) The phlebotomist can locate no accessible veins.

D) All of the above

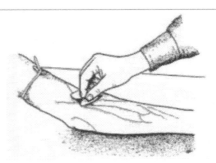

After venipuncture, a piece of cotton can be pushed down to the procedure's site to stop the bleeding. The vein will try to close the puncture as soon as possible.

Which of the following can be the reason for applying additional pressure to the site of venipuncture to stop the bleeding?

A) Low blood pressure

B) Intake of anticoagulants

C) Long-term intake of aspirin

D) Both B and C

Hemochromatosis refers to high iron count.

Sclerotic refers to the veins that are hardened from repeated blood draws.

Plasmapheresis is the process of removing blood plasma from whole blood.

A cannula is a tubular instrument used in patients with kidney disease to gain venous blood access for dialysis.

Hemoconcentration is the excessive accumulation of blood into an area of the body, usually caused by a tourniquet left on too long.

How many of the terms about venipuncture given above is defined correctly?

A) 2
B) 3
C) 4
D) 5

Capillary puncture is becoming famous in the medical field. Its advantages, as well as being a less invasive procedure, adds more popularity to it.

Which of the following is contained in capillary puncture blood?

A) Venous blood
B) Arterial blood
C) Interstitial fluids
D) All of the above

Reflux is a process of flowing back up to a source or origin. Acid reflux happens from the stomach, which may cause heartburn.

Which of the following would likely allow reflux during venipuncture?

A) The tourniquet is released early.
B) Filling the tube stopper end first
C) Lateral redirection of the needle
D) Drawing blood in the wrong order

34

Sheena is a phlebotomist and was ordered to collect a sample from one patient.

Which of the following must she do if the patient's doctor is in the room and the specimen is STAT-ordered?

A) Ask the nurse what to do.

B) Say "Excuse me" and continue to collect the sample.

C) Wait for the doctor to leave before entering the room.

D) Introduce herself politely, state the reason why she is there, and ask consent to proceed.

35

A phlebotomist is performing a **partial thromboplastin time (PTT)** on a patient with problematic veins. However, he was able to draw only partial tubes in all his attempts.

Which of the following actions should he take in this case?

A) Collect the sample specimen by skin puncture.

B) Have another phlebotomist try to get a specimen.

C) Mix the contents of the two tubes in a separate tube.

D) Send the tubes to the laboratory with a note that the patient has problematic veins.

36

Sodium citrate is a salt used to precipitate calcium, which is essential for blood coagulation. Precipitated calcium can be in its non-ionized form or as an insoluble oxalate.

Which color tubes is used for the samples that contain sodium citrate?

A) Blue

B) Green

C) Purple

D) Orange

37

Andy, a patient in the hospital, has several short-length IV-type tubings protruding from his chest.

Which of the following most likely pertains to these tubes?

A) CVC

B) Port

C) PICC

D) A-line

CONTINUE ▶

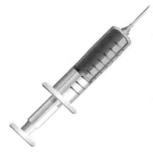

## 38

Needles are the primary equipment used in drawing and collecting blood samples. Different types and sizes of needles are used for various tasks.

Which of the following states the purpose of using multi-draw needles?

A) They are used to get blood samples from multiple patients at one time.

B) They are used to collect blood samples from multiple patients at multiple times.

C) They are used to draw one tube of the blood sample from one patient multiple times.

D) They are used to get multiple tubes of blood samples from one patient during venipuncture.

## 39

When conducting tests for a blood specimen, the results must be based on the laboratory technicians' findings. The healthcare professionals will then refer these results to the normal reference range to infer the patient's illness.

Which of the following does the "normal reference range" refer to?

A) Sick patients

B) Healthy individuals

C) People of the same age range

D) People with the same symptoms as the patient

40

During venipuncture, it is advised to avoid hitting nerves to lessen the complications of the procedure. An angry, unwilling patient must not be agitated further by failing to conduct the venipuncture properly.

Which of the following is the effect on the patient if a phlebotomist hits a nerve during venipuncture?

A) Swelling of the skin
B) Sharp radiating pain
C) Internal hemorrhage
D) It does not have any effect.

41

A winged infusion set is a tool used for venipuncture, specifically for accessing a superficial vein. This device is also known as a scalp vein or butterfly.

Which of the following equipment is part of a winged infusion set?

A) Two flexible wings
B) Hypodermic needle
C) Transparent tubing
D) All of the above

42

The **chain of custody documentation** refers to the chronological process of documenting a piece of physical or electronic evidence. Some hospital tests require this type of documentation as a well-kept record.

Which of the following tests may require special chain-of-custody documentation when the specimen is collected?

A) TDM
B) Drug screen
C) Blood alcohol
D) Blood culture

## 43

Fasting is a medical request for a patient to endure lacking intake of either food or liquid (like water or juice). This procedure is given for a patient to follow for the tests that he/she may undergo.

Which of the following tests are most affected if the patient is not fasting?

A) Electrolytes and bilirubin

B) Glucose and triglycerides

C) CBC and prothrombin time

D) Blood culture and cardiac enzymes

The phlebotomist must follow the standard procedures and be cautious of any complications of venipuncture.

Which of the following is the vein of choice for a venipuncture?

A) Basilic vein

B) Cephalic vein

C) Radial cubital

D) Median cubital

The order of draw recommends that blood samples should be placed in specimen tubes in the right order to avoid clotting or contamination.

Which of the following illustrates the proper order of the tubes?

A) Blood culture tubes, anticoagulated tubes, coagulation tubes

B) Coagulation tubes, anticoagulated tubes, blood culture tubes

C) Tubes without anticoagulant additives, other anticoagulated tubes, coagulation tubes, blood culture tubes

D) Blood culture tubes, coagulation tubes, other anticoagulated tubes, tubes without anticoagulant additives

## 46

Blood clots are gel-like clumps of blood that can prevent excessive bleeding. If a clot forms inside your veins, it won't always dissolve on its own, and if it travels to the brain, it may cause a severe health problem.

Which of the following about blood clots is correct?

A) A thrombus is a blood clot that forms inside one of your veins or arteries.

B) An embolus is a thrombus that breaks loose and travels from one location in the body to another.

C) Fibrin, a protein in blood clots, creates a web-like structure that binds together platelets and red and white blood cells at the injury site.

D) All of the above

47

A **thrombus** is a type of blood clot that stays in its original position. It may block or inhibit the blood flow in this region or channel if it grows too big.

Which of the following can imply that a thrombus had formed in the artery while collecting an ABG?

A) The site forms hematoma quickly.
B) The patient complains about excessive pain.
C) The pulse distal to the site is very weak.
D) All of the above

48

How can a phlebotomist identify their respective inpatients before drawing blood samples from them?

A) Confirming from the patient's relative
B) Looking at the hospital room number and bed assignment
C) Asking the patient's name and looking at the number on the hospital bracelet
D) None of the above

49

The phlebotomist must carefully draw blood according to the prioritization.

Which of the following is the order of drawing blood by a dermal puncture for bilirubin, blood smear, and Complete Blood Count (CBC)?

A) Blood smear, bilirubin, CBC
B) Blood smear, CBC, and bilirubin
C) CBC, bilirubin, and blood smear
D) CBC, blood smear, and bilirubin

50

The arterial insertion angle for the needle is essential to avoid hitting the other side of the arterial wall. Puncturing through two sides will let the artery bleed more and may cause some complications in the procedure.

Which of the following is an acceptable angle of needle insertion for radial ABGs?

A) 15 degrees
B) 30 degrees
C) 45 degrees
D) 55 degrees

51

Capillary blood sampling, obtained through a puncture, is a less invasive procedure than venous blood sampling. It is used on the earlobes, heels, or fingers.

Which of the following is not equipment for a capillary puncture?

A) Lancelet

B) Gauze pad

C) Povidone-iodine pad

D) Microcollection device

52

Emmett was tasked to collect a 5-mL blood sample from an 18-month old baby confined in the pediatric ward.

Which of the following veins should he choose as the collection site?

A) Basilic vein

B) Cubital vein

C) Dorsal hand vein

D) Median cubital vein

53

A phlebotomist must be licensed to be able to perform venipuncture on a patient. The patient has the right to receive proper care from the healthcare institution in which he/she is situated.

Which of the following is committed by a phlebotomist who performs an arterial puncture that caused damage to the patient without authorization?

A) Assault

B) Forced

C) Unethical

D) Malpractice

54

Which of the following substances in the blood dramatically increases with any changes in the position?

A) Iron

B) Glucose

C) Cortisol

D) Testosterone

55

To obtain the best capillary specimen using the finger, align the puncture device perpendicular to the fingerprint's whorls. The phlebotomist should avoid the finger's tip because puncturing the fingertip may cause unnecessary discomfort to the patient.

What will be the consequence if a phlebotomist fails to puncture across the fingerprint?

A) It will be challenging to collect the blood into the container.
B) The blood will not bead, but rather it will travel down the channels between the fingerprint lines.
C) Scraping the blood from the skin while filling the container will result in hemolysis and the specimen's clotting.
D) All of the above

56

There are different methods to locate veins. The most common medical tool to help find veins is a tourniquet.

Which of the following is a more prominent method to locate veins?

A) Hanging the arm down
B) Applying cold compress
C) Massaging the arms upward
D) Applying heat for at least 3 minutes

57

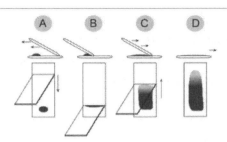

A **blood smear test** is a test that determines any abnormality in the blood cells of the patient. The test focuses on red and white blood cells and a few other blood cells.

Which of the following is the proper angle of the spreader slide when preparing a blood smear?

A) 15 degrees
B) 20 degrees
C) 30 degrees
D) 60 degrees

58

A government organization hosted a blood donation drive in a nearby village. Emily, a phlebotomist, volunteered to analyze the blood specimens obtained from the blood bank.

Which of the following color-stoppered tubes should she use?

A) Pink
B) Black
C) Green
D) Grey/Yellow Tiger Top

The Allen Test is the standardized method of assessing the blood supply in the hand artery. The test is used before planned intravascular access or patient selection for radial artery harvesting.

Which of the following is the Allen Test used for?

A) To assess if the artery is fragile or not.
B) To check if there is enough oxygen supply.
C) To determine if the artery is large enough.
D) To determine if collateral circulation is present.

Patients with chronic kidney disease (CKD) can develop kidney failure requiring dialysis to filter the blood. In hemodialysis, the patient's blood is filtered through an artificial kidney.

Hemodialysis is done with vascular access. Which of the following is a site of entry for hemodialysis?

A) Central venous catheter; a flexible tube (catheter) is put into a vein in the neck. It is an option if hemodialysis is needed very quickly.
B) An arteriovenous fistula (A-V fistula); An artery and vein are joined together under the arm's skin. It needs 6 weeks or longer to heal before it can be used for hemodialysis.
C) An arteriovenous graft (A-V graft); A plastic tube is used to join an artery and vein under the skin. It heals in only 2 weeks, so you can start hemodialysis faster.
D) All of the above

61

Larry was asked to collect a hemoglobin sample from a patient in the intensive care unit. However, the patient has an IV in his left arm and has no suitable hand or antecubital vein in his other arm.

Which of the following actions should Larry take?

A) Draw a hand vein below the IV.

B) Ask a colleague to gather the sample.

C) Attempt to collect the specimen from an ankle vein.

D) Get the sample by skin puncture on a finger of the right hand.

62

A patient suddenly begins to look pale, his eyes start to roll back into his head, and he complains of dizziness after the blood draw.

What action should the phlebotomist take?

A) Slap the patient gently

B) Lean the patient back in the chair.

C) Put a cold compress on the blood draw site.

D) Put a warm compress on the blood draw site.

63

Therapeutic drug monitoring refers to the medical practice of observing and determining the drug concentration or levels in the patient's body. A specific time is set for the monitoring to be determined on safe and optimal levels.

Which of the following defines TDM Peak Concentration?

A) Optimized concentration for maximum effectiveness

B) Preferred concentration for sub-optimal effectiveness

C) The highest concentration of the drug during a dosing interval

D) The lowest concentration of the drug during a dosing interval

64

Nicole was tasked to gather a blood specimen from an infant in the neonatal intensive care unit for a complete blood count. The infant, however, was crying and screaming.

Which of the following states why she should not collect a blood sample?

A) The blood sample will likely hemolyze.

B) The platelets in the infant's blood might clump.

C) The glucose level in the infant's blood might erroneously increase.

D) The white blood cells in the infant's blood may be incorrectly elevated.

CONTINUE ▶

An analyte is a substance that is to be analyzed in a hospital. It is usually measured and identified in the laboratory for medical purposes.

Which of the following is the analyte with a higher concentration when obtained through dermal puncture than venipuncture?

A) Glucose

B) Potassium

C) Active protein

D) Vitamin A and B

Inspecting the vein for the site of venipuncture is an integral part of the process. A vein is unlikely to be punctured if it is narrow and deep.

Which of the following is the reason for a vein to feel stiff and cord-like when palpated?

A) Fistula

B) Granulation

C) Vein Thrombosis

D) Vein to be too fragile

Which of the following might cause vein collapse during venipuncture?

A) The tourniquet is tightly placed.

B) The tube vacuum is too big for the vein size.

C) The tourniquet is near the venipuncture site.

D) All of the above

A phlebotomist notices the presence of **petechiae** (tiny red, flat spots that appear on the skin) on both patient's arms during the patient's examination.

What does this condition indicate?

A) Possible infectious disease

B) Possible clotting problems

C) Possible areas of inflammation

D) Possible blood pressure problems

As a phlebotomist, it is essential to verify the patient's condition through a skin check before doing a venipuncture. A patient that is ill enough may have to delay the procedure for another time.

Which of the following can be developed with a pale patient who has cold and damp skin?

A) Anemia

B) Sclerosis

C) Syncope

D) Coagulation problems

The history of **aspirin, also known as ASA or acetylsalicylic acid,** begins with its synthesis and manufacture in 1899. It is believed to be a harmless over-the-counter (OTC) drug that's been relied on for years to treat pain and fever.

Which of the following is correct about aspirin?

A) Daily low-dose aspirin is a blood-thinning medicine.

B) Low-dose aspirin helps prevent platelets from sticking together.

C) The treatment of thrombocythemia involves the use of low-dose aspirin.

D) All of the above

A blood alcohol test is a hospital test used to determine a patient's blood alcohol levels. Emergency patients are usually not able to use a breathalyzer, hence, a blood test.

Which of the following is acceptable to clean the arm with for a blood alcohol test?

A) Methanol

B) Iodine solution

C) Isopropyl alcohol

D) Benzalkonium chloride

Apheresis is a medical procedure to remove whole blood from a patient and separate the blood into individual components.

Which of the following about apheresis is correct?

A) It is also known as hemapheresis and pheresis. It originates from the Greek word "aphaeresis" which means "to take away".

B) It is often done on donors to obtain individual components such as platelets to use for transfusion in different patients.

C) During the process, some part of the blood such as platelets or white blood cells is taken out, and the rest of the blood is returned to the donor.

D) All of the above

Joshua, a phlebotomist, was asked to collect a blood sample from a patient and perform an electrolyte analysis as part of a routine health check-up.

What color tube must he use in the analysis?

A) Red

B) Green

C) Lavender

D) Light blue

Thrombin is an enzyme that plays a significant role in regulating blood coagulation and maintaining hemostasis. It works as a catalyst in the conversion of fibrinogen to fibrin, which is a fundamental step in clot formation.

When working with samples containing thrombin for STAT serum testing, which of the following tubes should be used?

A) Lavender

B) Light blue

C) Gold or Red/Black Tiger Top

D) Orange or Grey/Yellow Tiger Top

75

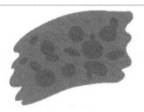

A blood draw forces the body to produce sufficient blood to function accurately, and this can be a cure or relief from some illnesses.

Which of the following is the illness that can be treated by removing a unit of blood without replacement?

A) Arthritis

B) Lung cancer

C) Polycythemia

D) Tuberculosis

76

Among the listed equipment used in venipuncture, which of the following can be used more than once?

A) Needles

B) Tourniquets

C) Tube holders

D) Collection tubes

77

The skin of the patient shows the signs of complications that may happen during venipuncture. Usually, healthy-looking skin will give a pass for the procedure, including the standard process of checking for venipuncture site.

When a phlebotomist applies a tourniquet, tiny red spots appear on the patient's arm. Which of the following is implied by these red spots?

A) The veins are narrow.

B) The patient is anemic.

C) The site may bleed excessively.

D) The veins are more in-depth than usual.

78

Venipuncture refers to the act of removing blood from a vein for laboratory testing. Blood samples are usually collected by puncturing the skin.

When performing a skin puncture, which of the following should a phlebotomist do with the initial drop of blood?

A) Wipe off the blood.

B) Hemolyze the blood.

C) Use the blood for the sample.

D) Keep the blood and store it for further use.

79

Blood specimens must be collected depending on the type of test that it will undergo. The site of the blood draw may also vary due to the requirement of the test.

Which of the following tests requires an arterialized specimen?

A) Glucose
B) Biliburin
C) Blood gases
D) Electrolytes

80

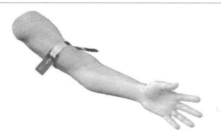

A **tourniquet** is used to pressure a limb or extremity to reduce or completely stop blood flow. This band is usually used during venipuncture and accidents.

Which of the following states the correct position of a tourniquet during a venipuncture procedure?

A) 3 inches above the venipuncture site
B) 3 inches below the venipuncture site
C) 2 inches above the venipuncture site
D) 2 inches below the venipuncture site

81

The phlebotomist must determine the vein to be used for venipuncture. The vein must be healthy and not fragile for the procedure to be successful, and cleaning must be done after venipuncture.

Which of the following should be done after cleaning the venipuncture site?

A) Allow the alcohol to completely dry.
B) Allow the alcohol to dry using the aircon.
C) Fan the alcohol for it to dry more quickly
D) Apply the alcohol, then wipe it afterward with cotton

82

A capillary puncture procedure is less painful as compared to a venous puncture. The needle used for a capillary puncture is smaller and shorter, but it is not used for collecting the blood specimen.

Which of the following is a proper capillary puncture procedure?

A) Wipe away the very first drop of blood.
B) Choose a site that has not been punctured too many times.
C) Determine whether a finger or a heel would be most appropriate for use.
D) All of the above

83

The hospital may require different tests upon the arrival of the specimen. The laboratory healthcare workers must measure the tests' priority levels accordingly to determine which patients must have their samples collected first.

Which of the following specimen must be collected first?

A) Timed glucose test
B) ASAP CBC in ICU
C) STAT glucose in the ER
D) STAT hemoglobin in ICU

84

The concentration of the different cells present in the blood specimen is vital to analyze the sample. The primary role of a phlebotomist is to ensure that the sample is well-drawn.

Which of the following can cause a decrease in plasma volume, hemoconcentration?

A) Clenching of fist
B) Excessive probing
C) Failing to clench the fist
D) Applying the tourniquet for more than one minute

85

Jasmin works in a hospital and analyses collected blood samples in red-stopper tubes.

Which of the following statements is correct about the blood samples?

A) The blood will not clot.
B) The blood samples produce plasma and cells.
C) The blood samples yield serum and clotted red cells.
D) The blood samples may be used for most coagulation tests.

86

A patient who undergoes critical or sensitive medication must have his/her blood monitored for medicine concentration. This kind of monitoring is upon the recommendation of the physician in charge.

Which of the following is the timeframe of collection of the trough level for therapeutic drug monitoring?

A) After the patient has fasted for 10 hours
B) Eight hours before the first intake of medicine
C) Thirty minutes after the medication is administered
D) Thirty minutes before the medication is administered

87

In some cases, phlebotomists do blind probing to locate a vein for venipuncture.

Which of the following can excessive or blind probing for a vein cause?

A) Lipemia
B) Nerve Damage
C) Diurnal Variation
D) Iatrogenic Anemia

88

Although it is hoped that no patient will have any ill-effects from the blood draw, it's relatively normal to have a small bruise at the venipuncture site.

Which of the following is the reason for developing a bruise?

A) A bruise might form if the phlebotomist does not apply enough pressure after removing the needle.
B) The patient is more likely to develop a bruise if the venipuncture procedure is more difficult than usual.
C) It usually appears because small blood vessels are accidentally damaged as the phlebotomist inserts the needle.
D) All of the above.

89

The **radial artery puncture** is a procedure that is performed for medical analysis of the blood specimen. A needle is punctured through the radial artery to satisfy the blood sample requirement.

Which of the following is the main use of an arterial puncture?

A) Evaluating blood gases
B) Determining electrolytes
C) Measuring calcium levels
D) Obtaining mineral samples

90

The physician must request that a venipuncture be performed to obtain blood from the patient. The phlebotomist will then act at the request of the physician rather than independently doing the procedure.

Which of the following veins requires a physician's approval for venipuncture?

A) Lower arm veins
B) Pediatric patients
C) Foot and leg veins
D) Diabetic patients

91

Children are naturally scared of needles due to different reasons, and venipuncture may be problematic for pediatric patients.

Which of the following may be required while performing venipuncture on a pediatric patient?

A) Assistance

B) Small evacuated tubes

C) Lock-on devices to pin the patient

D) All of the above

92

An **evacuated tube** is a type of vacuum tube that is mainly used for routine venipuncture. The tube is made of glass or plastic to contain the blood specimen from a patient.

Which of the following may happen for using an evacuated tube whose expiration date has passed?

A) Clotted samples

B) Insecure gel barriers

C) Incompletely filled tubes

D) All of the above

93

If a patient is severely allergic, which of the following substances must a phlebotomist always be cautious about?

A) Latex

B) Perfume

C) Adhesive bandages

D) None of the above

94

Arterial Blood Gases are the gases present in the blood tested and determined through the blood obtained from an arterial puncture. The blood gases can be harmful depending on their volume in the blood.

Which of the following are supplies included in arterial blood draw?

A) Tourniquet

B) 18-gauge needle

C) Heparinized syringes

D) All of the above

95

Phlebotomists use some of the equipment or apparatus in exceptional circumstances. These items are required for patients who have difficulties with the procedure.

Which of the following patient is a bariatric phlebotomy chair designed?

A) Paralyzed
B) Mentally ill
C) Overweight
D) Overfatigued

96

Maria was assigned to collect a blood sample from a diabetic patient. After gathering the blood sample, she noticed that the collection site continues to bleed after five minutes.

Which of the following actions must she take?

A) Inform the doctor or nurse.
B) Wrap a pressure bandage on the collection site.
C) Put a bandage on the side and tell the patient to hold pressure over the dressing.
D) None of the above.

97

The blood in the human body contains some gases that can be used to determine if such gases are causes of the illness of the patient. The arterial puncture is the method used to obtain blood for the test.

Which of the following is the main artery of choice for the procedure?

A) Ulnar artery
B) Radial artery
C) Brachial artery
D) None of the above

98

Analytes in the blood can be measured on different levels depending on the patient's time and diet intake. The phlebotomist must ensure that the blood drawn is in line with the test conducted on the specimen.

Which of the following analytes has its peak levels at 8:00 in the morning?

A) Glucose
B) Cortisol
C) Bilirubin
D) Eosinophil

A phlebotomist must examine a patient's skin and read his body conditions before drawing blood. The patient may fall ill, or the blood draw may cause complications if done wrong.

Which of the following is the term for tiny red spots appearing on a patient's skin?

A) Syncopia
B) Hemolysis
C) Petechiae
D) Hemoconcentration

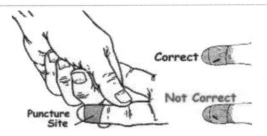

If there is no need to obtain a good amount of blood from a patient, a dermal puncture may be recommended instead of a venipuncture. The dermal puncture is more appropriate if you only need a drop or two.

For which of the following patients is the dermal puncture a better option?

A) Diabetic patients
B) Geriatric patients
C) Chemotherapy patients
D) All of the above

Robi needed to perform STAT potassium, partial thromboplastin time, and complete blood count on a blood sample.

If he was to follow the order for a multi-tube draw, which of the following is the correct order of the tubes he should use?

A) Gold top, yellow top, light blue top
B) Royal blue top, yellow top, gold top
C) Light blue top, green top, lavender top
D) Lavender top, green top, light blue top

The evacuated tube system (ETS) is the standard equipment used for routine venipuncture.

Which of the following is an essential part of the Evacuated Tube System (ETS)?

A) A tube holder
B) A needle device
C) An air evacuated tube
D) All of the above

103

David, a phlebotomist, is collecting a specimen by venipuncture. He heard a hissing sound while there was a spurt of blood afterward.

Which of the following must have happened?

A) The vein burst.
B) The needle is too deep.
C) The vacuum tube escaped.
D) The tube contents provoked reflux.

104

In some cases, phlebotomists have a hard time collecting blood samples from patients.

Which of the following devices is used as an alternative if blood samples are not drawn using conventional techniques?

A) BD Unopette
B) Butterfly needle
C) BD Microtainer
D) Heparinized Natelson tube

105

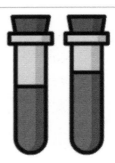

Blood samples are obtained with the recommendation of a physician as well as the permission of the patient. Some cases do not allow a healthcare worker to acquire a blood sample from the patient for a while.

Which of the following reasons can stop a healthcare worker from collecting blood from a patient's arm?

A) Mastectomy
B) Fragile veins
C) Small and narrow veins
D) Blood has a transmittable disease.

106

Phlebotomists are obligated to clean the chosen venipuncture site using 70% alcohol before puncturing the skin.

Which of the following describes the proper cleansing of the collection site?

A) Circular motions from the center to the edge of the site
B) Circular motions from the center to the point of injection
C) Circular motions from the center to the opposite side of the starting point
D) Any movement is acceptable.

107

One way of collecting blood samples is by puncturing a finger. Conventional finger puncture technique includes all EXCEPT which of the following points?

A) Avoid robust massaging.

B) Prick the ring or middle finger.

C) Clean or wipe away the first drop of blood.

D) Puncture aligned with the fingerprint whorls.

108

Which of the following states why phlebotomists usually collect blood samples from infants using their dorsal hands rather than skin puncture?

A) The dorsal hand requires fewer punctures to get blood.

B) Hemolysis occurs more often when doing skin punctures.

C) The specimen is less diluted if skin puncture is performed.

D) Getting blood samples from the dorsal hand is less stressful for an infant.

109

A blood serum specimen is collected as a liquid that is left after the blood clots. Centrifugation will separate the supernatant from the blood clots.

Which of the following cannot be used to collect a serum specimen?

A) SST

B) PST

C) Red stopper tube

D) Orange stopper tube

110

Phlebotomists must write laboratory reports that indicate all the procedures done and results obtained in a particular test conducted.

Why should a report form specify that a blood specimen has been collected by skin puncture?

A) For insurance and liability reasons

B) Other test results vary depending on the sample source

C) So that the succeeding samples will be collected by the same method

D) So that the nurse will know and check if the site has signs of infection

As children tend to be scared of a blood draw, the phlebotomist must ensure that the child is secured to be immobile during the process. The guardian or parents are usually the ones to help the phlebotomist in holding the child if needed.

Which of the following is the least effective way of immobilizing a child for a blood draw?

A) Getting help from an immobilizer

B) Firmly holding the child's arm in a palm-up position

C) Letting the child sit on a lap to hold him firmly in a sitting position

D) Allowing the child to sit with one arm bracing his other arm while you draw blood

The radial artery is the most prominent artery for the Arterial Blood Gas (ABG) test, which measures the acidity, pH, and oxygen levels.

Which of the following is correct about radial artery?

A) It is on the thumb side of the wrist.

B) It is less likely to cause a hematoma during the procedure.

C) A phlebotomist should palpate the radial artery but should not apply a tourniquet.

D) All of the above

CONTINUE ▶

SECTION 3 VENIPUNCTURE

#	Answer	Topic	Subtopic	#	Answer	Topic	Subtopic	#	Answer	Topic	Subtopic	#	Answer	Topic	Subtopic
1	A	TC	S3	29	D	TC	S3	57	C	TC	S1	85	C	TC	S3
2	C	TC	S3	30	D	TC	S2	58	A	TC	S3	86	D	TC	S1
3	B	TC	S1	31	D	TC	S1	59	D	TC	S1	87	B	TC	S2
4	C	TC	S1	32	D	TC	S1	60	D	TC	S1	88	D	TC	S2
5	B	TC	S1	33	B	TC	S2	61	D	TC	S2	89	A	TC	S1
6	B	TC	S1	34	D	TC	S1	62	B	TC	S2	90	C	TC	S1
7	A	TC	S2	35	B	TC	S2	63	C	TC	S1	91	D	TC	S1
8	C	TC	S3	36	A	TC	S3	64	D	TC	S2	92	D	TC	S3
9	B	TC	S1	37	A	TC	S2	65	A	TC	S1	93	A	TC	S2
10	D	TC	S2	38	D	TC	S3	66	C	TC	S2	94	C	TC	S1
11	C	TC	S1	39	B	TC	S2	67	D	TC	S2	95	C	TC	S2
12	B	TC	S1	40	B	TC	S2	68	B	TC	S2	96	A	TC	S2
13	C	TC	S1	41	D	TC	S3	69	C	TC	S2	97	B	TC	S1
14	A	TC	S1	42	C	TC	S1	70	D	TC	S1	98	B	TC	S2
15	C	TC	S1	43	B	TC	S2	71	D	TC	S1	99	C	TC	S2
16	D	TC	S2	44	D	TC	S1	72	D	TC	S1	100	D	TC	S1
17	B	TC	S1	45	D	TC	S1	73	B	TC	S3	101	C	TC	S1
18	D	TC	S3	46	D	TC	S1	74	D	TC	S3	102	D	TC	S3
19	C	TC	S2	47	C	TC	S1	75	C	TC	S1	103	C	TC	S2
20	D	TC	S2	48	C	TC	S1	76	B	TC	S3	104	B	TC	S3
21	C	TC	S3	49	B	TC	S1	77	C	TC	S2	105	A	TC	S2
22	D	TC	S2	50	C	TC	S1	78	A	TC	S1	106	A	TC	S1
23	D	TC	S3	51	C	TC	S3	79	C	TC	S3	107	D	TC	S1
24	C	TC	S2	52	C	TC	S1	80	A	TC	S1	108	B	TC	S1
25	B	TC	S1	53	D	TC	S1	81	A	TC	S1	109	B	TC	S3
26	A	TC	S1	54	A	TC	S2	82	D	TC	S1	110	B	TC	S1
27	D	TC	S1	55	D	TC	S1	83	C	TC	S1	111	D	TC	S1
28	B	TC	S2	56	B	TC	S2	84	D	TC	S2	112	D	TC	S1

Topics & Subtopics

Code	Description	Code	Description
SC1	Routine Venipuncture	SC3	Venipuncture Equipment
SC2	Venipuncture Complications	TC	Venipuncture

CONTINUE ▶

TEST DIRECTION

DIRECTIONS

Read the questions carefully and then choose the ONE best answer to each question.

Be sure to allocate your time carefully so you are able to complete the entire test within the testing session. You may go back and review your answers at any time.

You may use any available space in your test booklet for scratch work.

Questions in this booklet are not actual test questions but they are the samples for commonly asked questions.

This test aims to cover all topics which may appear on the actual test. However some topics may not be covered.

Studying this booklet will be preparing you for the actual test. It will not guarantee improving your test score but it will help you pass your exam on the first attempt.

Some useful tips for answering multiple choice questions;

- Start with the questions that you can easily answer.

- Underline the keywords in the question.

- Be sure to read all the choices given.

- Watch for keywords such as NOT, always, only, all, never, completely.

- Do not forget to answer every question.

CONTINUE ▶

1

A patient may give informed consent after the nurse or physician explains what may happen during a procedure.

Which of the following does informed consent mean?

A) The patient has the right to look at all his or her medical records and test results.

B) The patient agrees to a procedure after being told of the consequences associated with it.

C) The nurse has the right to perform a procedure on a patient even if the patient refuses.

D) The phlebotomist explains to the patient why the test is ordered and the meaning of the results.

2

A blood chemistry test determines the amount of some specific chemicals in the blood. The test is used to determine if there are excessive or too low amounts of chemicals that may have caused an illness.

Which of the following electrolytes can be measured in the standard chemistry tests performed by POCT (Point-of-care testing) instruments?

A) Na and K

B) Hgb and Hct

C) PT and PTT

D) T4 and TSH

3

BBP is the abbreviation used for which of the following terms?

A) Blood-Borne Plasma
B) Blood-Borne Pathogen
C) Blood-Borne Prothombrin
D) None of the above

4

AABB: American Association of Blood Banks
AHIP: America's Health Insurance Plans
CDC: Centers for Disease Control and Prevention
CMS: Centers for Medicare and Medicaid Services
NCHS: National Center for Health Statistics
NHIS: National Health Interview Survey

How many of the acronyms about Health Care Structure given above are correct?

A) 3
B) 4
C) 5
D) 6

5

Which of the following is not a laboratory test that helps assess integumentary system disorders?

A) C&S
B) BUN
C) KOH prep
D) Skin biopsy

6

Proxemics is the general study of how humans use space in their surroundings. Psychological issues and communication patterns can be observed in this field.

Which of the following is an example of proxemics?

A) Eye contact
B) Living space
C) Zone of comfort
D) Facial expressions

## 7

In medical terminology, the distances can be approximated by referring to a general description without an exact measurement. These terms are used since the point that being discussed has differences in its position depending on the patient's constitution and history.

Which of the following does the term "proximal" refer to?

A) Near the middle

B) Farthest to the middle

C) A little bit away from the middle

D) Nearest to the point of attachment

Which of the following is not a laboratory analysis that would help in checking for muscle disorders?

A) AST

B) C&S

C) Aldolase

D) Troponin

A blood vessel injury refers to the vessel's injury due to external stimuli such as a car crash, a bone fracture, etc.

Which of the following is the correct sequence of events after blood vessel injury?

A) Fibrinolysis, platelet adhesion, vasoconstriction

B) Platelet aggregation, vasoconstriction, fibrin clot formation

C) Vasodilation, platelet adhesion, fibrin clot formation

D) Vasoconstriction, platelet aggregation, fibrin clot formation

## 10

Which of the following about **belonephobia** is correct?

A) It is an abnormal fear of sharp or pointed objects such as needles.

B) It is derived from the Greek word "belone" meaning needle, and "phobos" meaning fear.

C) It is often also associated with the pathological fear of blood loss and, therefore, blood tests' fear.

D) All of the above.

11

A phlebotomist may be responsible for performing a variety of other duties.

Which of the following is among the duties of a phlebotomist?

A) Performing quality control testing and various clinical and clerical duties.
B) Performing point-of-care testing (POCT) such as blood glucose monitoring.
C) Transporting other specimens such as arterial blood and urine to the laboratory for testing.
D) All of the above.

12

Microbiology is a branch of biology that deals mainly with microscopic organisms. Such microorganisms include bacteria, germs, viruses, and fungi.

Which of the following is performed by the microbiology department?

A) Compatibility testing
B) Electrolyte monitoring
C) Culture and sensitivity testing
D) Enzyme-linked immunoassay

## 13

AB- (away from): abnormal; away from the normal

HYPER-(excessive): hyperglycemia; excessive blood sugar levels

PARA-(beside): parathyroid; beside the thyroid gland

PERI-(around): pericardium; membrane around the heart

PRE-(before) prenatal; before birth

POST-(after) post-surgical stage; stage after surgery

SUB-(under) submucosa; tissue below mucus membrane

Meanings of some prefixes are explained above, and examples are given. How many of them are explained correctly?

A) 4
B) 5
C) 6
D) 7

## 14

In phlebotomy, the abbreviation GTT stands for which of the following?

A) Glucose Test Tube
B) Glucose Tolerance Test
C) Glucose Treatment Test
D) Glucose Tolerance Treatment

15

Nonverbal communication includes overall behaviors.

Which of the following practices help a phlebotomist gain a patient's trust?

A) Avoiding the patient's personal space
B) Maintaining erect body posture with relaxed arms.
C) Maintaining eye contact with the patient during the procedures.
D) All of the above

16

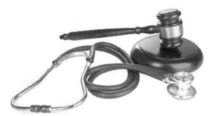

What is the basis for most medical malpractice suits?

A) Felonies
B) Misdemeanors
C) Criminal actions
D) Unintentional torts

17

A patient is to undergo a glucose tolerance test. The fasting specimen is drawn by 8:15, and the beverage is finished at 8:20.

Which of the following is the time for collecting the 1-hour specimen?

A) 9:20
B) 9:45
C) 9:50
D) 10:30

18

David was sued for the negligence of hiring an inexperienced phlebotomist last summer. The patient has been harmed due to the procedure performed by the phlebotomist.

Which of the following refers to this case?

A) Res ipsa loquitur
B) Vicarious liability
C) Assault and battery
D) The statute of limitations

CONTINUE ▶

19

Due care is the standard of care where a reasonable person would exercise under similar circumstances. It is also called **ordinary care** and **reasonable care.** The health care workers must provide due care to the patients entirely and professionally.

Which of the following is caused by failure to exercise "due care"?

A) Assault

B) Battery

C) Negligence

D) Malpractice

20

As a healthcare professional, it is a must that you will be able to deal with difficult patients. Providing excellent care to patients and being polite is a definite trait that must be developed in this field.

Which of the following is a proper telephone technique?

A) Being careful of the tone of your voice when answering the phone

B) Waiting for the phone to ring three or four times to appear less anxious

C) Listening carefully but not writing anything down to save time

D) Not identifying yourself to the caller in case there is a problem later.

21

Which of the following terms refers to a bacterial infection in the bloodstream resulting in blood poisoning?

A) Anemia

B) Leukemia

C) Ketonemia

D) Septicemia

22

Normal anatomical position is the body orientation used when describing an organism's anatomy.

Which of the following about the anatomic position for the body is correct?

A) Standing erect

B) The head facing forward

C) The arms by the sides with the palms facing to the front

D) All of the above

23

The patient has the right to reject the care necessary for him/her to be back in good health. The healthcare institute must acknowledge this but can try again to convince the patient.

Which of the following should be done by a phlebotomist who encounters a patient refusing a blood draw?

A) Ask another expert to collect the sample.
B) Ask the nurse for instructions about what happened.
C) Document the refusal and submit it to the physician
D) Both B and C

24

Micro-hematocrit tubes are thin capillary tubes used to measure the volume percentage of red blood cells in the blood.

What anticoagulant is added in a red-banded microhematocrit tube?

A) EDTA
B) Heparin
C) Sodium citrate
D) Potassium oxalate

25

Nonverbal communication does not involve speaking.

Which of the following refers to the legal term for a person touching a patient who shows nonverbal actions of permission?

A) Negligence
B) Paralanguage
C) Implied consent
D) Forced approval

26

Helen is a phlebotomist who breached the duty of care to a patient.

Which of the following is the exact term used to describe Helen's situation?

A) Assault
B) Civil action
C) Dereliction
D) Direct cause

CONTINUE ▶

27

The patient must be informed that he/she may undergo a test beforehand. Preparing the patient for a test is required to be able to obtain prior consent.

Which of the following manual describes the necessary steps to follow inpatient preparation for laboratory tests?

A) The Test Catalog
B) The Safety Manual
C) The Patient Record
D) The Procedure Manual

28

Blood is a specialized fluid that has several functions vital for human survival. It has four main components: red blood cells, white blood cells, platelets, and plasma.

Which of the following description about the components of blood is incorrect?

A) White blood cells form effective defenses against infections.
B) Plasma is the liquid component of blood and is composed of 70% water.
C) Red blood cells are responsible for carrying oxygen to and from the lungs.
D) Platelets are the cells that interact with clotting proteins to prevent or halt bleeding.

29

Which of the following organizations has the responsibility of mandating the quality assurance programs?

A) National People's Action (NPA)
B) American Society for Clinical Pathology (ASCP)
C) Occupational Safety and Health Administration (OSHA)
D) Joint Commission on Accreditation of Healthcare Organizations (JCAHO)

30

Which of the following organizations can certify a phlebotomist?

A) AMT: American Medical Technologists
B) ASCP: American Society for Clinical Pathology
C) ASPT: The American Society of Phlebotomy Technicians
D) All of the above

31

The four major blood type groups are A, B, AB, and O. A patient's blood group is entirely determined by the parent's genes, either from the father or the mother.

Which of the following determines an individual's blood type by its presence or absence in the red blood cell?

A) Antigens

B) Hormones

C) Antibodies

D) Minerals and nutrients

32

Medical malpractice often happens when a healthcare professional neglects the procedure, leading to endangering the patient's life. Some cases can be sent to the court depending on the degree of the malpractice.

Which of the following conforms to avoiding malpractice litigation?

A) Reporting incidents within 48 hours

B) Obtaining a signed consent for blood collection

C) Participating in national medical activities at least three times a year

D) Properly handling all of the patient's information in a confidential manner

33

Hepatitis refers to a condition in which a part of the body is inflamed, commonly caused by a viral infection.

Which of the following is the definition of Hepatitis?

A) Skin disorder

B) Cellular injury

C) Kidney infection

D) Liver inflammation

34

A blood culture test lets the physician know if there are harmful microorganisms like bacteria or germs in the patient's blood. The blood culture will show contamination if such presence is detected.

Which of the following departments have blood culture contamination as a quality indicator?

A) Microbiology Department

B) Disease-control department

C) Infection control department

D) Environment protection department

CONTINUE ▶

35

Which of the following tests is usually collected by venipuncture and should not be collected by dermal puncture?

A) Glucose
B) Blood cultures
C) Platelet counts
D) Complete blood count (CBC)

36

Glands in the body can eject or produce both good and harmful substances from the body. These glands help the body regulate the number of minerals that it can contain or serve as the body's tool to produce other bodily functions.

Which of the following are sudoriferous glands?

A) Connected to hair follicles
B) Referred to as sweat glands
C) Endocrine system structures
D) Responsible for goosebumps

37

A blood disorder is any health condition in which something is wrong with part of the blood.

Which of the following about the blood disorders given below is not true?

A) Multiple myeloma is a type of cancer that forms in plasma cells.
B) Polycythemia is a disorder involving the overproduction of red blood cells.
C) Lymphoma is a condition of deficiency of red blood cells or of hemoglobin in the blood.
D) Hemophilia is a bleeding disorder that causes severe bleeding from even a slight injury.

38

A phlebotomist is a specialist who specifically draws blood from the patient. This healthcare professional ensures that the blood drawing process is secure and safe for the patient.

Which of the following may be a duty of the phlebotomist?

A) Perform POCT
B) Analyze specimen
C) Chart patient results
D) Diagnose a patient's disease

CONTINUE ▶

The spinal cord and the brain are the central nervous system processors. The spinal cord helps transmit the signals to the brain while the brain helps the body act on it.

Which of the following are the protective membrane of the brain and spinal cord?

A) Neurons
B) Papillae
C) Meninges
D) Viscera

A patient's information is always considered confidential. The patient has the right to disallow individuals to obtain his/her information without prior consent.

Which of the following is the term for an unauthorized release of a patient's information?

A) Assault
B) Malpractice
C) Invasion of privacy
D) Invasion of secrecy

41

Fasting refers to abstaining from all kinds of food and drink for a certain length of time. Some laboratory tests require that a patient must fast for at least 8 hours before testing.

Which of the following states the purpose of ordering a fasting laboratory test?

A) To limit the patient's calcium level before testing

B) To remove the effects of the patient's diet on the test results

C) To keep the patient from feeling sick during the blood collection

D) To make the test results more consistent on a wide range of patients

42

What is the term used to refer to medical information that is linked to a specific patient?

A) Private health information

B) Protected health information

C) Protected confidential information

D) Confidentially protected information

43

Angelina collects the blood and then realizes that the blood collection site continues to bleed after 5 minutes.

Which of the following should Angelina do?

A) She has to wrap a pressure bandage around the site.

B) She must notify the patient's physician or nurse immediately.

C) She has to bandage the site and tell the patient to hold pressure over the bandage.

D) None of the above

44

Which of the following terms refers to independent laboratories that analyze samples from other healthcare facilities?

A) Waived labs

B) Reference labs

C) Urgent care centers

D) Physician office labs

45

The management of risk involves a lot of aspects, especially in a hospital. From the owners to the healthcare workers, the briefing and training must be ensured to run the hospital properly.

Which of the following can identify trends for risk management?

A) Test menus

B) Delta checks

C) External reports

D) Safety identification manual

46

In phlebotomy, ACD is an anticoagulant and was formerly used as a blood preservative.

Which of the following does ACD stand for?

A) Acid-Citrate Dextrose

B) Acid-Calcium Dextrose

C) Acid-Chloride Dextrose

D) None of the above

47

The management of a healthcare institute must ensure the overall systematic flow of the business. It is a must that the institute offers the standards of being able to provide decent healthcare to the patients by using advanced equipment and hiring professionals.

Which of the following is protected by the policies developed by the risk management department?

A) Patient

B) Employee

C) Healthcare professionals

D) All of the above

48

Which of the following suffix is not defined correctly?

A) -OMA: tumor

B) -PATHY: disease

C) -ECTOMY: a science of

D) -AEMIA : a condition of blood

49

OSHA defines **workplace violence** as any act or threat of physical violence, harassment, intimidation, or other threatening disruptive behavior at the workplace.

Which of the following is the leading factor of the violence in hospitals, nursing homes, and different healthcare settings?

A) The lack of armed security guards

B) Patients who are angry with the staff

C) Frustrated employees who hate their jobs

D) The diversity of people who can enter a healthcare facility any time

50

Doctors recommend the ESR test to some patients to provide an accurate diagnosis that causes inflammation, like arthritis, cancer, and autoimmune diseases.

The term ESR stands for which of the following?

A) Erythrocyte System Rate

B) Erythrocyte Sodium Rate

C) Erythrocyte Separation Rate

D) Erythrocyte Sedimentation Rate

51

Bloodborne diseases are infections carried in the blood by viruses or bacteria. People with these diseases may experience fatigue, nausea, and abdominal pains, while some might not experience any symptoms.

Which of the following bloodborne diseases can be transmitted by needle-stick?

A) Hepatitis C

B) Hepatitis D

C) Tuberculosis

D) Chagas disease

52

A phlebotomist must ensure that he/she maintains a hygienic standard as he/she undergoes different procedures in a healthcare institute.

Which of the following is not observed by a phlebotomist who fails to change gloves and wash hands between patients?

A) Patient's Bill of Rights

B) Joint Commission Patient Safety Goals

C) College of American Pathology Safety Rules

D) Clinical Laboratory Improvement Amendments

53

Which of the abbreviations about Nationwide Organisations is correct?

A) NHSN: National Healthcare Safety Network

B) NFPA: National Fire Protection Association

C) NASH: The National Surveillance System for Healthcare Workers

D) All of the above

54

Healthcare insurance can help the patient ease the burden on the financial aspect of being hospitalized. Subsidies are usually provided depending on the contribution amount you have applied for the insurance.

Which of the following refers to state and federally funded insurance?

A) ACO

B) HIPAA

C) Medicare

D) Medicaid

55

Regulatory agencies have been created to promote and develop a standard in clinical and laboratory testing. Different countries can adopt various regulations accordingly.

Which of the following laboratory regulatory agencies classifies laboratory tests by their complexity?

A) JC

B) CMS

C) CAP

D) HIPAA

56

Which of the following books or manuals should be consulted when a question concerning the principle behind a particular specimen collection arises?

A) Floor book

B) Policy manual

C) Procedure manual

D) Quality control logbook

57

Which of the following are phlebotomists allowed to earn through continuing education programs once they have been certified?

A) CEUs

B) A degree

C) Accreditation

D) Licensing points

58

CARDIO- heart	CYTO- cell
DERMA- skin	HISTIO- tissue
HEPATI- liver	MALIGN- harmful
NEPHRO- kidney	NEURO- nerves
OSTEO- bone	PAED- child
SARCO- tissue	TOXO- poison

Meanings of some root words are given above. How many of them are correct?

A) 7

B) 8

C) 10

D) 12

59

A **tort** is a wrongful act or an infringement of a right committed by one person against another that gives rise to injury or harm.

Which of the following about tort is correct?

A) Torts are classified as intentional and unintentional.

B) Negligence and malpractice are considered unintentional torts.

C) Assault, battery, and defamation are considered intentional torts.

D) All of the above.

60

Privacy

A patient's information is a private document that must be protected by the hospital. The document can be handed to the authorities upon request as long as it is legally acquired.

Which is the law that specifically addresses the privacy of health information?

A) Patient's Bill of Rights

B) JC Patient Safety Goals

C) Clinical Laboratory Improvement Amendments

D) Health Insurance Portability and Accountability Act

61

A phlebotomist must acknowledge a patient's rights according to the Patient's Bill of Rights. The hospital must accommodate the patient in line with the principles of being a healthcare provider.

Which of the following is not included in a phlebotomist's involvement in the Patient's Bill of Rights?

A) Respectful care

B) Refuse Treatment

C) Examine their hospital bill

D) Receive diagnostic information from their health-care provider

62

Arteries and **veins** are the two primary types of blood vessels in the human body. Arteries are the blood vessels that carry oxygen-rich blood away from the heart to the other parts of the body. On the other hand, veins are the blood vessels responsible for carrying deoxygenated blood from the body to the heart.

How many layers are the arteries and veins made of?

A) 1

B) 2

C) 3

D) 4

63

Which of the following medical term is used to refer to the inflammation of the liver?

A) Myositis

B) Nephritis

C) Hepatitis

D) Myocarditis

64

White blood cells (WBCs) are the immune system cells responsible for protecting the body against infections by fighting viruses, bacteria, and other foreign microorganisms. These cells are produced in the bone marrow but are circulated throughout the body.

How many types of white blood cells are present in the blood?

A) 5

B) 6

C) 7

D) 8

65

Which of the following terms describes the situation where patients donate their blood for use during their surgery?

A) Platelet donation

B) Autologous donation

C) Cryoprecipitate donation

D) Fresh frozen plasma donation

66

Which of the following types of muscle tissue is characterized by non-striated muscles and involuntary movement involved in hemostasis?

A) Skeletal muscle tissue

B) Smooth muscle tissue

C) Striated muscle tissue

D) Epithelial muscle tissue

67

Which of the following is the meaning of the suffix -emia?

A) Tumor

B) Paralysis

C) Opening

D) Blood condition

68

In the early days, bloodletting can become complicated due to possible infections that can happen to the donor. The lack of sterile medical equipment and diagnosis made it fatal to many.

Which of the following is not a piece of early equipment used for bloodletting?

A) Needle

B) Leach

C) Lancet

D) Hemostat

69

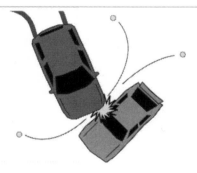

An accident refers to an unforeseen incident that often leads to injuries and damages.

Which of the following violations is protected when a healthcare professional provides emergency aid at an accident?

A) Oral consent

B) Implied consent

C) Expressed consent

D) Informed expressed consent

70

After passing a board examination, the passer has the right to use the title associated with it. Licensed/Registered Nurse can be attached as 'RN.'

Which of the following are the initials of the title granted after the successful completion of the American Society for Clinical Pathology phlebotomy examination?

A) PBT

B) MDP

C) CPT

D) LMP

71

Which of the following references should outline the duties and performance levels that are required of a phlebotomist?

A) Floor book

B) Safety manual

C) OSHA guidelines

D) Policies and procedure manual

CONTINUE ▶

72

The **endocrine system** is a regulatory system for different hormones produced by the body. The system releases hormones depending on the need of the body.

Which of the following is involved in the evaluation of the endocrine system?

A) Drug monitoring
B) Blood gas studies
C) Spinal fluid analysis
D) Hormone determinations

73

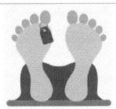

As healthcare professionals, it is a life's oath to help the sick recover their health. The patient must also be willing to undergo treatment for the sake of being back to good health.

Which of the following is the term for an unexpected patient death not related to the patient's illness?

A) Human error
B) Sentinel event
C) Root cause error
D) Professional liability

74

In hospitals, the nurses may usually take your temperature using Centigrade or degree celsius. Usually, the reason is the preference, and there is no need to get a more sensitive measurement like Fahrenheit.

Which of the following is the degree celsius equivalent of 77 degrees Fahrenheit?

A) 20
B) 25
C) 30
D) 40

75

Pulmonary diseases are commonly seen in people all over the world. It is usually reported as asthma, coughs, and other similar illnesses.

Which of the following is the organ affected by pulmonary diseases?

A) Ears
B) Lungs
C) Heart
D) Kidneys

CONTINUE ▶

76

The human blood comprises white blood cells, red blood cells, platelets, and plasma. Plasma, the liquid part of the blood, contains water, proteins, and salts, while the other three components comprise the solid part.

How many percent of the blood volume does the solid part of the blood make up?

A) 35%

B) 45%

C) 55%

D) 65%

77

A blood vessel can have various names as it grows larger in diameter. The location may also indicate its uses and the carrying capacity of the vessel.

Which of the following is the term used for the internal space of a blood vessel?

A) Valve

B) Lumen

C) Interior wall

D) Anterior space

78

Which of the following about the medical terminology with suffixes is not correct?

A) Blood terms end in -emia.

B) A breaking down is -lysis.

C) Pain terms end with -algia.

D) Breathing terms end with -opathy.

79

Proximity which means nearness or closeness refers to the distance between individuals they prefer when interacting with others.

Which of the following is not right about proximity?

A) You must ask permission to enter a patient's personal space.

B) You can introduce yourself after coming in closer proximity to the patient's bedside or chair.

C) Many patients can feel uncomfortable when a phlebotomist approaches them and enters their personal space.

D) Proximity or appropriate distance for personal space varies based on gender, culture, and personal preference.

80

The dermal puncture minimizes the amount of blood taken from the patient. An adequate blood collection from a dermal puncture may not be possible if a patient is dehydrated or has poor peripheral circulation.

Which of the following blood vessels is used to perform dermal (skin) punctures?

A) Veins

B) Arteries

C) Arterioles

D) Capillaries

81

A suffix is a morpheme that is added to create a derivative of a word. It makes different meanings after the new term is formed.

Which of the following can be true for a suffix?

A) It is placed before the root word.

B) It is attached after the root word.

C) It is placed in between the root word.

D) It creates a better definition of the root word.

82

Leuko- is a prefix originating from the Greek letter "leukos"

Which of the following colors is referred to by the prefix leuko-?

A) Red

B) Blue

C) White

D) Yellow

83

"Insufficient blood-clotting cells" is a severe health condition.

Which of the following refers to this case?

A) Hypovolemia

B) Erythrocytopenia

C) Thrombocytopenia

D) Thrombophlebitis

84

Which of the following terms refers to the body's early morning condition wherein the patient fasts and discontinues exercise for approximately 12 hours?

A) Basal state
B) Basal lamina
C) Basal ganglia
D) Basal metabolic rate

85

Which of the following is the triangle-shaped cavity located in the elbow joint, which contains the median nerve, a tendon of the biceps, and the brachial artery?

A) Iliac fossa
B) Radial fossa
C) Acetabular fossa
D) Antecubital fossa

86

A **blood culture bottle** is used as a medical apparatus to determine bacteria or fungi' presence in the bloodstream. The blood and the media must be diluted appropriately for the results to show up correctly.

Which of the following is the amount of blood that must be added to 45 mL media to complete a 1:10 dilution?

A) 5 mL
B) 8 mL
C) 11 mL
D) 15 mL

87

What is the expected volume of blood of an average adult in liters?

A) 1 to 2 liters
B) 7 to 8 liters
C) 3 to 4 liters
D) 5 to 6 liters

88

Which of the following substances has a higher value in capillary blood as compared to venous blood?

A) Calcium
B) Potassium
C) Total protein
D) Hemoglobin

89

Hepatitis is a disease that causes inflammation and damage to the liver. People with hepatitis experience fatigue and flu-like symptoms and have yellow eyes and skin.

Which of the following types of hepatitis cannot be transmitted by blood?

A) Hepatitis A
B) Hepatitis B
C) Hepatitis C
D) Hepatitis D

Medical term or medical terminology refers to the language used to precisely describe the parts of the human body and procedures performed.

Which of the following is the correct order of arrangement in identifying a medical term?

A) Word root + Suffix + Prefix

B) Suffix + Prefix + Word root

C) Suffix + Word root + Prefix

D) Word root + Prefix + Suffix

Consent is the agreement of both parties to conduct testing or any other activities.

Which of the following refers to the act of touching a patient without consent?

A) Assault

B) Detention

C) Extortion

D) Battery

CONTINUE ▶

92

ID bands are worn on the hospital to verify the identity of the patient. This measure is made for safety and security reasons in the hospital.

Which of the following is the best thing to do when the patient's ID band lacks the information you need for collecting specimens?

A) Use the name on the door.

B) Refuse to draw the specimen and cancel the request.

C) Ask the patient's name and collect the specimen if it matches the requisition.

D) Ask the patient's nurse to put an ID band on the patient before you draw the specimen.

93

Health care professionals commonly use a list of abbreviations and other medical terminology to search and record information and give instructions rapidly.

Which of the following medical abbreviation is defined correctly?

A) ER: Emergency room

B) EBL: Estimated blood loss

C) H&H: Hemoglobin and hematocrit

D) All of the above

94

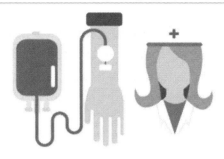

Phlebotomists refer to trained professionals to collect blood from a patient, mostly from veins, for clinical testing, transfusions, or research.

Luke, a phlebotomist, wants to look at his friend's lab result for curiosity. Which of the following law will he violate?

A) WHO: World Health Organization

B) DMAS: Department of Medical Assistance Services

C) HIPPA: Health Insurance Portability and Accountability Act of 1996

D) CLIA: The Clinical Laboratory Improvement Amendments of 1988

95

The **statute of limitation**s set the period for bringing up legal actions towards crime or case. The period depends on the case, the state, or the country.

When can the statute of limitation's timing begin?

A) On the day the negligent act took place

B) A month after the injury was discovered

C) The first day of consulting with a lawyer

D) The first day in a series of medical treatments

96

Phlebotomy's early use was referred to as a procedure known as **bloodletting**, which was believed to return the body to a balanced state.

Which of the following about bloodletting is true?

A) It was believed to eliminate any diseases from the body and to reduce fever.

B) It is the withdrawal of blood from a patient to prevent or cure illness and disease.

C) It used a process called "venesection," which pierces the vein with a sharp object to drain blood.

D) All of the above.

97

A patient is called upon to undergo treatment after the method, risks, and consequences are explained. The patient agrees to it afterward.

Which of the following does the case above belong to?

A) Implied consent

B) Informed consent

C) Preferred consent

D) Verbal consent

98

In phlebotomy, the abbreviation PT indicates which of the following tests?

A) Platelet time

B) Pregnancy test

C) Prothrombin time

D) Partial thromboplastin

99

The concentration of different substances in the blood, like minerals and nutrients, can be the indicators in the health of the patient as well as possible causes of the illness and disease.

Which of the following substances has a higher concentration in capillary blood than in venous blood?

A) Glucose

B) Calcium

C) Nitrogen

D) Total protein

CONTINUE ▶

100

Which of the following references would help a phlebotomist determine the turn-around time for any specific procedure?

A) Floor book
B) Patient's chart
C) Policy manual
D) Physician's Desk Reference

101

The CLIA Rules and Regulations introduce the clinical and laboratory standards that must be met when handling specimens such as blood, saliva, muscles, tissues, bones, etc.

Which of the following administers the CLIA federal regulations?

A) CMS
B) CAP
C) CLSI
D) CoW

102

Which of the following means the cause or origin of a disease or disorder?

A) Etiology
B) Cytology
C) Histology
D) Immunology

103

Which of the following lists the four elements of negligence?

A) Injury, liability, tort, malpractice
B) Tort, privacy, direct cause, injury
C) Deleriction, duty, injury, direct cause
D) Contract, litigation, confidentiality, felony

104

What department is responsible for identifying pathogenic microorganisms in patient samples and the analysis of culture and sensitivity tests?

A) Virology department
B) Mycology department
C) Parasitology department
D) Microbiology department

105

Blood is the transport fluid in animals and humans responsible for delivering essential substances, such as oxygen and nutrient, to the body's cells and carrying away waste products, such as carbon dioxide. The amount of blood in the body depends on body weight.

If an average adult weighs around 150 to 160 pounds, which is the amount of blood in his/her body?

A) 1 liter
B) 2 to 3 liters
C) 4 to 6 liters
D) 7 to 8 liters

106

Which of the abbreviations about the tubes used by phlebotomists is correct?

A) SSTs: Serum separator tubes
B) PSTs: Plasma separator tubes
C) PPTs: Plasma preparation tubes
D) All of the above

107

Who among the experts given below is responsible for studying the causes and development of a disease, specifically diagnosing a condition based on the laboratory analysis of bodily fluids, and is usually the one who gives direction and oversees the laboratory?

A) Pathologist
B) Pharmacist
C) Phlebotomist
D) Medical assistant

108

Diseases that can be spread via blood and body fluids are not only limited to AIDS/HIV.

Which of the following diseases can also be spread with blood and other bodily fluids?

A) Hepatitis C
B) Hepatitis B
C) Alzheimer's disease and Hepatitis C
D) Hepatitis B and Hepatitis C

109

You have a cancer patient named Tom. His mother arrived and handed you a gift check amounting to $30.

Which of the following should you do in response?

A) Courteously return the gift to the mother.

B) Accept the gift and use it to buy pizza for the unit.

C) Accept the gift and provide extra care to Tom as gratitude.

D) Return the gift and request the mother to recommend you for a salary increase instead.

110

A medical test that characterizes clotting is called **activated partial thromboplastin time (APTT)** or **partial thromboplastin time (PTT)**. Historically, it was known as the **Kaolin cephalin clotting time (KccT)**.

Which of the following is being monitored by APTT tests?

A) Chemotherapy

B) Physical therapy

C) Heparin therapy

D) Warfarin therapy

111

The **lymphatic system** is a vital part of the immune system. It is part of the circulatory system made of a network of lymphatic vessels that carries a clear fluid known as lymph directionally towards the heart.

Which of the following body part does not belong to the lymphatic system?

A) Liver

B) Spleen

C) Tonsils

D) Thymus

112

The .... requires all workplaces, including healthcare settings, to have security plans for the prevention of workplace violence.

Which of the following completes the statement given above?

A) National Institutes of Health

B) Health Insurance Portability and Accountability Act

C) Occupational Safety and Health Administration

D) The Centers for Disease Control and Management

CONTINUE ▶

SECTION 4 BASICS OF PHLEBOTOMY

#	Answer	Topic	Subtopic	#	Answer	Topic	Subtopic	#	Answer	Topic	Subtopic	#	Answer	Topic	Subtopic
1	B	TA	S5	29	D	TA	S2	57	A	TA	S2	85	D	TA	S2
2	A	TA	S3	30	D	TA	S3	58	D	TA	S4	86	A	TA	S4
3	B	TA	S4	31	A	TA	S2	59	D	TA	S5	87	D	TA	S2
4	D	TA	S1	32	A	TA	S5	60	D	TA	S5	88	D	TA	S4
5	B	TA	S2	33	D	TA	S4	61	C	TA	S5	89	A	TA	S2
6	C	TA	S5	34	A	TA	S5	62	C	TA	S2	90	B	TA	S4
7	D	TA	S2	35	B	TA	S4	63	C	TA	S4	91	D	TA	S5
8	B	TA	S2	36	B	TA	S2	64	A	TA	S2	92	D	TA	S3
9	D	TA	S2	37	C	TA	S2	65	B	TA	S1	93	B	TA	S4
10	D	TA	S3	38	A	TA	S5	66	B	TA	S2	94	C	TA	S5
11	D	TA	S3	39	C	TA	S2	67	D	TA	S4	95	A	TA	S5
12	C	TA	S5	40	C	TA	S5	68	D	TA	S5	96	D	TA	S3
13	D	TA	S4	41	B	TA	S3	69	B	TA	S5	97	A	TA	S5
14	B	TA	S4	42	C	TA	S1	70	A	TA	S5	98	C	TA	S4
15	D	TA	S3	43	B	TA	S3	71	D	TA	S2	99	A	TA	S2
16	D	TA	S2	44	B	TA	S1	72	D	TA	S2	100	A	TA	S2
17	C	TA	S3	45	A	TA	S5	73	B	TA	S5	101	A	TA	S5
18	A	TA	S5	46	A	TA	S4	74	B	TA	S4	102	A	TA	S4
19	C	TA	S5	47	D	TA	S5	75	B	TA	S4	103	C	TA	S2
20	A	TA	S5	48	C	TA	S4	76	B	TA	S2	104	D	TA	S1
21	D	TA	S4	49	D	TA	S5	77	B	TA	S2	105	C	TA	S2
22	D	TA	S2	50	D	TA	S4	78	D	TA	S4	106	D	TA	S4
23	D	TA	S5	51	A	TA	S2	79	B	TA	S3	107	A	TA	S1
24	B	TA	S4	52	B	TA	S5	80	D	TA	S4	108	D	TA	S3
25	C	TA	S5	53	D	TA	S4	81	B	TA	S4	109	A	TA	S5
26	C	TA	S2	54	D	TA	S5	82	C	TA	S4	110	C	TA	S1
27	A	TA	S5	55	B	TA	S5	83	C	TA	S2	111	A	TA	S2
28	B	TA	S2	56	C	TA	S2	84	A	TA	S4	112	C	TA	S5

Topics & Subtopics

Code	Description	Code	Description
SA1	Health Care Structure	SA4	Medical Terminology
SA2	Human Anatomy & Physiology	SA5	Legal & Ethics
SA3	Introduction to Phlebotomy	TA	Basics of Phlebotomy

CONTINUE ▶

TEST DIRECTION

DIRECTIONS

Read the questions carefully and then choose the ONE best answer to each question.

Be sure to allocate your time carefully so you are able to complete the entire test within the testing session. You may go back and review your answers at any time.

You may use any available space in your test booklet for scratch work.

Questions in this booklet are not actual test questions but they are the samples for commonly asked questions.

This test aims to cover all topics which may appear on the actual test. However some topics may not be covered.

Studying this booklet will be preparing you for the actual test. It will not guarantee improving your test score but it will help you pass your exam on the first attempt.

Some useful tips for answering multiple choice questions;

- Start with the questions that you can easily answer.

- Underline the keywords in the question.

- Be sure to read all the choices given.

- Watch for keywords such as NOT, always, only, all, never, completely.

- Do not forget to answer every question.

1

Which of the following about the fire safety procedures is correct?

A) The most common type of fire extinguisher is a Class ABC.
B) The acronym RACE should be followed when a fire is first discovered.
C) The acronym PASS should be followed when operating a fire extinguisher.
D) All of the above

2

How frequently should 10% bleach be prepared if it is going to be used as a cleaning agent?

A) Every day
B) Every week
C) Every 3 hours
D) Every 6 hours

3

A tube additive serves as a catalyst for the blood specimen in the tube to react in a way or another. Some tests directly involve the addition of such additives to obtain results.

Which of the following is the correct angle of degrees to mix the additives by turning off the wrist and back again?

A) 60 degrees
B) 90 degrees
C) 180 degrees
D) 270 degrees

4

Which of the following is not monitored by arterial blood collection?

A) Glucose
B) Ammonia
C) Lactic acid
D) Blood gases

Blood culture tests are used to determine if there are microorganisms, especially harmful ones, in your bloodstream. The test requires a blood culture bottle to be used for the collected blood specimen.

Which of the following is the most critical part of blood culture collection?

A) Collecting bottle
B) A mixture in the vial
C) Antisepsis of the collection site
D) Timing of the second set of culture

6

The **glucose tolerance test** is a method used to assess the body's capacity to process glucose. It detects Type 2 Diabetes and Gestational Diabetes.

Which of the following actions of a patient is not a restriction for conducting a glucose tolerance test?

A) Eating fruit
B) Chewing gum
C) Drinking water
D) Drinking coffee

## 7

Blood samples must be collected according to the indications and restrictions of the test performed on it. These samples must be drawn using the standard and appropriate method for the test.

Which of the following tests require the blood sample to be protected from the light?

A) CBC
B) Bilirubin
C) Blood smear
D) HIV-AIDS

8

In determining the illness of a patient, different types of tests can be conducted according to the preliminary findings of the attending physician. Some tests are unique, while some are commonly used for specimen analysis.

Which of the following is the specimen used to conduct a Guaiac Test?

A) Blood
B) Feces
C) Saliva
D) Sweat

9

Evacuated tubes are containers that are vacuum-like inside. The specimen is stored properly in the tube where there are no contaminants present.

Which of the following causes evacuated tubes to fill with blood automatically?

A) Arterial blood pressure

B) Venous blood pressure

C) Premeasured tube vacuum

D) External pressure from a device

10

A phlebotomist enters the patient's room to collect blood, but the patient is sleeping.

Which of the following should the phlebotomist do in this case?

A) Postpone the blood collection.

B) Wait until the patient wakes up.

C) Report the issue to the supervisor.

D) Wake up the patient gently and allow him/her to become oriented.

11

If a chemical substance is accidentally spilled on your body or on the patient's body, which of the following is the first thing you have to do?

A) Notify your supervisor

B) Clean the area with water

C) Refer to the Material Safety Data Sheet (MSDS)

D) Quickly neutralize the chemical with Isopropyl alcohol

12

What needle size is suitable for a child younger than two years?

A) 18 gauge needle

B) 21 gauge needle

C) 23 gauge needle

D) 25 gauge needle

13

The principle of radiation safety is "**ALARA.**" ALARA stands for "as low as reasonably achievable." It means that even if it is a small dose, if receiving that amount has no direct benefit, you should try to avoid it.

Which of the following is the guiding principle of radiation safety?

A) Time

B) Distance

C) Shielding

D) All of the above

14

A simple way of avoiding the spread of infections is by hand washing or hand hygiene.

Which of the following steps is not part of the proper handwashing procedure?

A) Wash the hands for at least 15 seconds.

B) Wet the hands with water before putting on a soap.

C) Step back so that the clothing does not touch the sink.

D) Turn off the faucet using the towel used to dry the hands.

CONTINUE ▶

15

Which of the following diseases is the most commonly occurring laboratory-attained infection?

A) Hepatitis B

B) Hepatitis C

C) Tuberculosis

D) Acquired Immune Deficiency Syndrome

16

Newborn (neonatal) screening tests look for developmental, genetic, and metabolic disorders in the newborn baby.

According to United States national program of newborn screening tests, which ailments must be screened by neonatal screening tests?

A) PKU and hypothyroidism

B) PKU and hyperthyroidism

C) PKU and sickle cell anemia

D) PKU and biotinidase deficiency

17

John has an elderly patient that wants to go back to bed.

Which of the following acts is proper non-verbal communication?

A) Sitting in the room's chair

B) Helping the patient go to bed

C) Collecting the phlebotomy equipment

D) Assessing the patient's medical records

18

A **chain of reaction** refers to the sequence of events that allow microorganisms to cause specific infections in an individual.

Which of the following points is a factor that increases a host's vulnerability to a microorganism?

A) Drug use

B) Vaccination

C) Proper nutrition

D) Use of disposable apparatus

The electrolytes in the body act as a natural substance to inhibit or promote different bodily systems such as energy storage or the loss of fluids and fats. The body loses electrolytes through various means, like sweating excessively during physical workouts.

Which of the following test uses sweat electrolytes to diagnose?

A) RSC

B) AIDS

C) Peptic ulcers

D) Cystic fibrosis

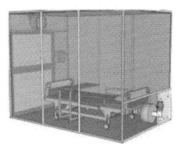

An **isolation room** is a special room in a hospital where patients with infectious and easily transmitted diseases are placed. The room is maintained to hold and isolate the patient from other patients so that the disease does not transmit.

Which of the following must a phlebotomist do first before entering an isolation room?

A) Wear PPE

B) Show your entry permit

C) Perform personal hygiene

D) Read the posted instructions

21

Phoebe was asked to gather a blood specimen from a patient with an enteric pathogen in the emergency room.

Which of the following precautions should she use?

A) Droplet

B) Contact

C) Airborne

D) Standard

22

Hemolysis is the medical term given to the process of the red blood cell's breakdown. The different tinges of red appear after a blood specimen is centrifuged.

Which of the following results in specimen hemolysis?

A) Using a tourniquet to hold the last tube

B) Filling the blood tubes at a random angle

C) Using anticoagulants on the blood specimen

D) Using a large-volume tube with a 23-gauge needle

23

Cold agglutinins are antibodies produced by a person's immune system. **Cold agglutinin disease (CAD)** is a rare autoimmune disorder described by the premature destruction of red blood cells.

Which of the following is true about the cold agglutinin sample collection procedures?

A) Collect specimen in a red top tube; do not use SST tube, keep the sample at room temperature, and transport blood immediately to the laboratory.

B) Centrifuged at 37 degrees Celcius, and separate serum from red cells within one hour of collection.

C) Do not refrigerate before the separation of serum from red cells. Store separated serum in the refrigerator.

D) All of the above

24

Povidone-iodine is an antiseptic used to disinfect the skin before and after surgery to prevent infection.

Using this solution for cleaning the patient's skin may interfere with analyzing which of the following elements?

A) Glucose
B) Bilirubin
C) Creatinine
D) Cholesterol

25

Feces, also called stool, are the solid or semisolid remains of food that could not be digested in the small intestine.

Which of the following tests feces for parasites?

A) Oncology
B) Hematology
C) Microbiology
D) Immunology

26

Universal Precautions is a medical practice introduced in the late 1980s to protect healthcare professionals from infections.

Which of the following states the fundamental principle of Universal Precautions?

A) Patients in isolation wards are the only ones considered infectious.
B) The most critical bloodborne pathogen is the Human Immunodeficiency Virus (HIV).
C) Laboratory coats and gloves give adequate protection from blood and other body fluids.
D) The body fluids and blood of all individuals are treated as if they are contagious or infectious.

27

MSDS or a **material safety data sheet** is a report that contains all the necessary information on the plausible health effects of exposure to chemicals and the procedures on how to handle hazardous substances.

Which of the following materials should have a material safety data sheet?

A) Isotonic saline
B) Isopropyl alcohol
C) Most patient medications
D) Fluid-resistant laboratory coats

28

HBV, HCV, and **HIV** cause Hepatitis B, Hepatitis C, and acquired immunodeficiency syndrome (AIDS), respectively. All diseases are potentially life-threatening as they target vital organs in the body, such as the liver and the immune system.

Through which of the following methods are these pathogens transmitted?

A) Injuries involving sharp objects
B) Making contact with non-intact skin without wearing gloves
C) Contact of body fluids and blood with the mucous membranes
D) All of the above

## 29

Hospitals are large medical institutes that may contain indefinite amounts of pathogens that may cause infection or diseases. This is why the hospitals place significant importance on the cleanliness of the surroundings to avoid such mishaps.

Which of the following is referred to by the terms "HAI" and "Nosocomial"?

A) Contacted by visitors

B) Contacted by patients

C) Contacted by medical practitioners

D) Contacted by the surrounding population

What point-of-care test is used for monitrong heparin therapy?

A) PT or APTT

B) ACT or APTT

C) ACT or PT

D) PT or TT

Jimmy will be performing a skin puncture on a 20-year old patient. As a phlebotomist, which of the following fingers should he choose as the blood collection site?

A) Little finger

B) Index finger

C) Middle finger

D) Any finger can be a collection site

The arterial blood gas values are obtained through the processing of the blood specimen in the laboratory. The results may be wrong due to different reasons, from the specimen collection to the conducting of the test.

Which of the following can cause erroneous ABG values?

A) Analysis delay for more than 30 minutes

B) Inadequate mixing results in microclots

C) Presence of air bubbles in the specimen

D) All of the above

33

A **trace element-free tube** is used for isolating the element traces in the blood of the patient. The lack of contamination of trace elements in the tube helps determine the elements present in the blood.

Which of the following tests need such a collection tube?

A) CBC
B) ABGs
C) Aluminum
D) Electrolytes

34

Semen specimens must be clean and unpolluted. The specimen must be appropriately stored during and after collection.

Which of the following should not be followed in the collection of a semen specimen?

A) Collect from a condom
B) Record the time of collection
C) Place in a warm and sterile container
D) Abstain from sexual activity within a period of 3-5 days

35

A POCT can be done at home or at a healthcare institute. Hospitals often allow patients to undergo testing at other medical diagnostics centers if applicable.

Which of the following POCT tests can be done both at home and the hospital?

A) Glucose
B) Bilirubin
C) Electrolytes
D) Complete Blood Testing

36

Sodium polyanethole sulfonate, or SPS, is a component of a culture media used in growing bacteria from a blood sample drawn from patients with suspected bacteremia cases. This ingredient primarily hinders bacteria destruction through various humoral and cellular factors.

If a phlebotomist works with blood samples containing SPS, which of the following tubes should they use?

A) Pink
B) Purple
C) Dark blue
D) Light yellow

37

Colon cancer is both preventable and highly treatable when detected early. Colonoscopy every ten years starting at age 45 or 50 is a suggested screening option.

Which of the following tests is suitable for screening colon cancer?

A) Glucose
B) Cholesterol
C) Occult blood
D) Hemoglobin

38

A **blood glucose test** is used to determine the sugar levels of a patient. This test is used in many other extensive tests, aiding in determining the illness of the patient.

Which of the following is the fasting time of a patient who needs to undergo a timed blood glucose test?

A) 3-4 hours
B) 4-6 hours
C) 6-9 hours
D) 8-12 hours

39

A pregnancy test can be via blood or urine. The most common method is using a pregnancy kit and doing a urine test.

Which of the following urine sample will be most appropriate for a pregnancy test?

A) Timed sample
B) Random sample
C) First few drops sample
D) Midstream clean-catch sample

147

CONTINUE ▶

40

Infections can be avoided by maintaining a clean environment. Washing of hands can help control the spread of disease or possibly eliminate them by following hygienic procedures.

In which of the following cases should a healthcare worker perform hand hygiene?

A) After putting on gloves
B) Before putting on gloves
C) When the gloves are soiled or used
D) All of the above

41

Material Safety Data Sheet (MSDS) is a document that lists information relating to occupational safety and health for the use of different substances and products.

Which of the following is correct about MSDS?

A) It provides information on sharps.
B) It provides information on patients.
C) It provides information on chemicals.
D) It provides information on office procedures.

42

Personal protection equipment (PPE) is an essential requirement for being a healthcare worker. It is crucial to protect the self before attempting to care for others.

Which of the following is a PPE?

A) Biohazard bag
B) Nonlatex gloves
C) Countertop cover
D) Sterile rubber bag

43

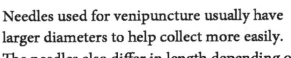

Needles used for venipuncture usually have larger diameters to help collect more easily. The needles also differ in length depending on the type of patient.

Which of the following needles has the largest diameter?

A) 18 gauge
B) 20 gauge
C) 23 gauge
D) 25 gauge

44

A **blood smear test** is conducted to detect any abnormalities present in your blood cells. This type of test is commonly seen in newborn screening.

Which of the following is the "pusher slide" angle when making a blood smear test?

A) 10 degrees
B) 15 degrees
C) 30 degrees
D) 50 degrees

45

Which of the following manifestations can be observed when someone has a reaction to latex?

A) Anaphylaxis
B) Allergic contact dermatitis
C) Irritant contact dermatitis
D) All of the above

46

The **Clinical & Laboratory Standards Institute (CLSI)** is an internationally recognized non-profit organization aiming to improve and foster excellence in laboratory medicine.

Which of the following is the CLSI's recommended order of draw?

A) Gray, light blue, green
B) Lavender, green, and gray
C) Orange, red, and light blue
D) Light blue, light green, and lavender

47

A prothrombin time or protime test (PT) is a test used to detect and diagnose signs of clotting or bleeding disorders in the body. The Internationalized Normal Ratio (INR) is a calculated value from a PT result to monitor medication like Coumadin Therapy.

Which of the following is not an error most commonly associated with incorrect PT (INR) results?

A) Inadequate application of the specimen

B) Using the first drop of dermal puncture blood

C) Failure to adequately cleanse and dry the capillary puncture site

D) Premature capillary puncture before test strip/cartridge is ready to accept the sample.

48

Blood transfusion is a process of intravenously transferring donated blood to save another person's life. This procedure is usually done on patients who lost blood from severe injuries or diseases. Although this process generally saves lives, it can also allow the transmission of infectious diseases.

Which of the following diseases is not transmitted through blood transfusion?

A) Syphilis

B) Hepatitis B

C) Diabetes mellitus

D) Human immunodeficiency virus

49

Which of the following sentences about the labeling of urine samples is true?

A) The urine sample must be labeled after collection.

B) The urine sample must be labeled before collection.

C) The urine sample must be labeled by the patient.

D) The urine sample must be labeled on the lid of the specimen.

50

The government lets the healthcare workers enjoy a safe and clean environment. By introducing laws and agreements with the medical institutes, these workers are given benefits that fit their work scope.

Which of the following mandates safe working conditions?

A) CDC

B) OSHA

C) HazCom

D) HICPAC

51

While preparing the equipment needed for venipuncture, Deanna accidentally stuck herself with a needle.

When should she report the accident?

A) Straight away

B) After her shift

C) Before her next shift

D) After consulting her physician

52

Phlebotomists always follow proper laboratory etiquette when analyzing in a laboratory.

Which of the following is not an appropriate laboratory safety procedure?

A) Always wear closed shoes.

B) Put hair away from the face.

C) Wear a laboratory gown at all times.

D) Never apply makeup, drink, or eat inside the laboratory.

53

Saliva, blood, and sweat can be carriers of microorganisms that can be harmful to the human body. These bodily fluids must be controlled, especially when the individual has illnesses that can be transmitted through these media.

Which of the following is the most appropriate action to take if a body fluid splashes to the eyes?

A) Call 911

B) Rub your eyes

C) Flush water to your eyes for 10 minutes

D) Wait for a medical healthcare worker to attend to you

54

It is common to see dried-up specimens on the countertop from time to time. Although the healthcare workers are vigilant towards cleanliness, it cannot be avoided that there are misses here and there.

Which of the following is a proper way to clean up a small blood spill that has dried on a countertop?

A) Wash it with soap and water

B) Use a disinfectant wipe to scrub the surface

C) Rub alcohol on the area and wipe it clean

D) Moisten it with a disinfectant and carefully absorb it with a paper towel

55

Nosocomial infections are diseases that are caught in a hospital and caused by antibiotic-resistant organisms.

Which of the following diseases has the highest prevalence of this type of infection?

A) Skin infections

B) Wound infections

C) Urinary tract infections

D) Respiratory tract infections

56

How many minutes before having an oral glucose tolerance test (OGTT) should a patient drink the glucose solution?

A) 5 minutes

B) 20 minutes

C) 30 minutes

D) 45 minutes

57

The human chorionic gonadotropin (HCG) test is done to check for the hormone HCG in blood or urine.

What condition is evaluated when the HCG levels are being determined?

A) Anemia

B) Pregnancy

C) Liver disease

D) Urinary tract infection

58

Inflammatory diseases include a vast array of disorders and conditions that are characterized by inflammation.

Which of the following inflammatory disorder is explained correctly?

A) Arthritis is the inflammation of the joints.

B) Cystitis is the inflammation of the bladder.

C) Phlebitis is the inflammation of a blood vessel.

D) All of the above

59

A person donating blood is subjected to limitations like alcohol consumption prohibition within the past few days. Other restrictions include the absence of tattoos and other body recreation that is semipermanent on the skin.

Which of the following is the gauge needle that is used for blood donation?

A) 10-14

B) 12-15

C) 16-18

D) 20-24

60

The order of draw determines the type of blood that is collected for the test. Usually, the preliminary tests can be placed first, while the least sensitive ones can be on the back of the order.

Which of the following is filled last in the recommended order of draw?

A) Red top

B) Lavender top

C) Light-blue top

D) Blood culture bottle

61

The hospitals are required to maintain a clean and safe environment for patients to recover from their diseases. One of the most critical aspects of this cleanliness is controlling the spread of diseases in the institute.

Which of the following situation involves a Healthcare-Associated Infection (HAI)?

A) A man has a kidney infection before admission

B) A healthcare worker contracts hepatitis B from a needle stick

C) A patient from surgery has an infection from the incision

D) A child in the ward has dengue fever but is not recovering

62

In conducting different tests for a blood specimen, the use of the necessary tools and equipment is crucial to guarantee the results' accuracy. Some tests require special apparatus to provide specific results.

Which of the following tests requires the blood specimen to be placed in circles on special filter paper?

A) ABGs

B) CBGs

C) Bilirubin

D) Phenylketonuria (PKU)

CONTINUE ▶

63

CLINICAL AND
LABORATORY
STANDARDS
INSTITUTE®

According to the standards set by the CLSI, how many failed venipuncture attempts can a single phlebotomist have on the same patient?

A) Up to 5

B) No more than 2

C) There is no limit

D) Decided by the medical facility

64

Most healthcare settings enable barcode specimen collection that uses three hardware components: a barcode scanner, a label printer, and a handheld device for viewing information. The collection process links a barcode on the patient's wristband with the orders in the LIS.

Which of the following should Katie, a qualified phlebotomist, do during the barcode specimen collection?

A) Scan her ID badge to log in and identify herself as the collector

B) Scan the patient's wristband and ask for a second identifier

C) Scan the labeled tubes again to confirm that the specimen labels match the patient.

D) All of the above

65

The **glucose tolerance test (GTT)**, also known as the **oral glucose tolerance test (OGTT)**, measures your body's sugar response, and your blood sugar level can give your doctor valuable clues about your health.

Which of the following is not true about GTT?

A) It measures the body's ability to metabolize glucose.

B) It is used primarily in the diagnosis of type II diabetes and gestational diabetes.

C) Its results depend only on the pancreas' capacity to produce insulin and the amount of 'active' insulin.

D) A measured dose of glucose is given by mouth to the fasting patient, and the glucose levels in the blood and urine are measured at intervals.

66

A healthcare worker must practice cleanliness at all times, especially in the hospital and work premises. Surgeries and other infection-related interactions must be paired with complete PPE (personal protection equipment).

Which of the following is the correct order of wearing PPEs?

A) Gown, gloves, mask

B) Gown, mask, gloves

C) Gloves, mask, gown

D) Mask, gown, gloves

67

Point-of-care testing refers to the place where a patient can undergo a test. The POCT can be at or near the hospital.

Which of the following must an operator secure to document in performing a POCT?

A) Patient's tests
B) Quality control
C) Electronic controls
D) All of the above

68

During a routine venipuncture, the phlebotomist must secure the order of draw depending on the test that the blood specimens may undergo. The color of the vacuum container's top can help indicate which tests such blood specimens may undergo.

Which of the following stopper color can a vacuum have to collect a serum specimen?

A) PST
B) Red stopper
C) Green stopper
D) Light-blue top

69

Joey collected a blood sample from one patient with a suspected case of diabetes. However, he noticed traces of blood on the outside of the tube that he just filled up with blood.

Which of the following procedures should he do?

A) Let the blood dry out.
B) Put a biohazard sticker on the tube.
C) Wipe the outside of the tube with a disinfectant.
D) Dispose of the tube and collect another blood sample.

70

Laboratory tests are required to be requested by an attending physician of the patient to help determine the patient's illness.

Which of the following is the best method for requesting a lab test?

A) Personal request
B) Electronic request
C) Handwritten request
D) Verbally transmitted request

71

Glycolysis is the chemical process of the breakdown of glucose. This process can take place with or without the presence of oxygen.

Which of the following additive prevents glycolysis?

A) EDTA

B) Heparin

C) Potassium Oxide

D) Sodium Flouride

72

David, a phlebotomist, was asked to collect a pleural fluid.

From which of the following areas must the sample be collected?

A) Joint

B) Chest

C) Arms

D) Heart

73

Six Sigma is a disciplined, data-driven approach for eliminating defects in any process. It is a methodology to improve the capability of any operation.

Which of the following refers to Six Sigma methodology?

A) Assessment of variables in a process

B) Assessment of errors and quality in an operational setting

C) A different way of quality assessment to control variables

D) Use of statistics to determine the variable and to reduce error

74

What test is going to be performed on a patient if he/she is required to fast for 12 hours before the test?

A) Blood culture

B) Blood donation

C) Glucose tolerance test

D) Therapeutic phlebotomy

75

What do you call the percentage of packed red blood cells in a specific volume of blood?

A) Hemoglobin
B) Red blood cell count
C) Packed cell volume (PCV)
D) Erythrocyte sedimentation rate

76

Which of the following type of arteries are usually used in performing the modified Allen test?

A) Radial and ulnar arteries
B) Brachial and ulnar arteries
C) Femoral and radial arteries
D) Radial and brachial arteries

77

Semen collection helps obtain more information about male factor infertility or provide sperm for the next treatment steps.

Which of the following practices is correct regarding semen collection?

A) It must be kept refrigerated.
B) It must be collected in a condom.
C) It must be obtained after eight days of abstinence.
D) It must be delivered to the laboratory within 30 minutes of collection.

78

EDTA (Ethylenediaminetetraacetic acid) is a chemical designed to hold on or bind some minerals and metals such as chromium, iron, lead, mercury, copper, aluminum, nickel, zinc, calcium, cobalt, manganese, and magnesium. The bounded substances are made to be safe for the body and can be removed later on.

Which of the following tubes contains EDTA?

A) White top tubes
B) Purple top tubes
C) Lavender top tubes
D) All of the above

CONTINUE ▶

79

Microorganisms gather in the different body parts of an individual. Bathing regularly and washing hands more often will help kill and reduce these harmful microorganisms in the body.

Which of the following soaps destroys transient microorganisms when washing hands?

A) Plain soap

B) Sulfuric soap

C) Antiseptic soap

D) All of the above

80

An **infection** occurs when a microbe enters the body and begins to multiply. The most common sources of infection are air, water, people, and food.

Infections that originate in hospitals are known as which of the following?

A) Neonatal Infections

B) Neocomial Infections

C) Nosocomial Infections

D) Nasalcomial Infections

81

The color of the vacuum tube stopper commonly indicates the type of test that the blood specimen will undergo. The tube stopper's order can help the phlebotomist determine the order of draw by placing them in the proper order beforehand.

Which of the following test do the lavender-top tubes usually undergo?

A) Chemistry test

B) Immunology test

C) Hematology test

D) Complete blood typing test

82

Although alcohol in urine has a relatively short detection window, usually less than a day, alcohol byproducts can be detected in a person's urine for up to three days after he/she has consumed his/her last drink.

Because of which of the following is alcohol testing of urine doubtful?

A) Urine test results may not correlate with blood alcohol levels.

B) If the specimen is uncapped, alcohol can evaporate quickly.

C) False-positive results can be obtained because of fermentation by bacteria.

D) All of the above.

83

A capillary puncture can be performed on the earlobes, heel, or fingers. When conducting the procedure on the fingers, a phlebotomist can use any of the five fingers.

Which of the following fingers is the best choice for a capillary puncture?

A) Index

B) Thumb

C) Middle

D) Ring or Pinky

84

A **procedural control** is a set-up designed to ensure that a study follows the intended result. Isolation between samples or specimens can be a type of procedural control.

Which of the following is the procedural control that verifies the test kit and added reagents?

A) Internal controls

B) Remote controls

C) Electronic controls

D) Professional controls

85

Disinfectants are chemicals used to remove or destroy any traces of potentially infectious microorganisms.

Among the listed substances, which of the following is used to disinfect tourniquets and items contaminated with blood?

A) Iodophors

B) Chlorine bleach

C) Hydrogen peroxide

D) 70% isopropyl alcohol

86

An occult blood test is a lab test used to check samples for hidden (occult) blood.

What body fluid is used when performing the occult blood test?

A) Feces
B) Serum
C) Plasma
D) Cerebrospinal fluid

88

What is the unit of the value from a hand-held hemoglobin analyzer?

A) g/mL
B) g/dL
C) kg/L
D) g/nL

87

The saliva of a patient contains different amounts of bacteria. In some cases, the saliva contains fungi and disease-causing germs ingested through food and other media.

Which of the following can be detected by using a sputum sample to be tested?

A) Strep throat
B) Endocarditis
C) Tuberculosis
D) Cystic fibrosis

89

Contamination refers to the presence of undesirable elements that leads to the corruption or spoilage of materials. Substances may be contaminated due to the presence of biological, physical, or chemical contaminants.

Which of the following actions can result in the contamination of a blood culture?

A) Applying antiseptic on the patient's skin
B) Letting the antiseptic dry for 30 seconds
C) Handling only the handle of the scrub device
D) Repalpitating a disinfected site before performing venipuncture

90

An **exposure control plan** is an outline that contains the employer's policy to protect their workers from contracting bloodborne infections.

Which of the following points is not a required part of an exposure control plan?

A) Guidelines of isolation
B) Exposure determination
C) Implementation methods
D) Communication of hazards

91

Infection control programs are the implemented policies that help healthcare facilities improve and monitor their practices.

Which of the following statements is the primary purpose of an infection control program?

A) Identify the source of contagious infections.
B) Protect patients from outside contamination.
C) Isolate infectious patients from other patients.
D) Avoid the spread of disease in a healthcare facility.

92

Which artery in the body is the most frequently used artery during ABG collection?

A) Radial artery
B) Dorsalis pedis
C) Femoral artery
D) Brachial artery

93

Tube additives are chemicals added to the blood collection tube to preserve, isolate, etc., the targeted mineral or nutrient in the blood. The blood collection tube will then produce the desired result, given that the procedures are followed properly.

Which of the following tube additives can preserve glucose?

A) Sodium citrate
B) Sodium heparin
C) Sodium fluoride
D) Sodium polyanethol sulfonate

CONTINUE ▶

94

A point-of-care testing center must obtain a minimum amount of equipment to run the day-to-day operations. Blood, urine, and fecal tests are the most common tests a medical diagnostic testing center can handle.

Which of the following POCT analyzer is used to perform metabolic chemistry panels?

A) I-STAT
B) BiliChek
C) Glucometer
D) CholesTech LDX

95

Which of the following actions should be taken when collecting and transporting cold cryofibrinogen and agglutinins samples?

A) Cryofibrinogen and agglutinins samples must be chilled before collection.
B) Cryofibrinogen and agglutinins samples must be transported on ice to the lab.
C) Cryofibrinogen and agglutinins samples must be warmed before collection and transported warm.
D) Cryofibrinogen and agglutinins samples must be transported at room temperature.

96

The rapid strep test is a fast antigen detection test widely used in clinics to diagnose bacterial pharyngitis caused by streptococci.

Which of the following streptococcus group is usually detected when a rapid strep test is being performed on a throat culture?

A) Group A
B) Group B
C) Group C
D) Group D

A **phlebotomist** is an individual qualified to draw blood from patients mainly for medical testing, donations, transfusions, or clinical studies. They conduct several tests on blood samples, depending on the purpose, and place each tested sample in specific tubes for easier identification of the tube contents.

Grey tubes contain which of the following substances?

A) Thrombin
B) Fluoride and oxalate
C) Sodium heparin and EDTA
D) Lithium and sodium heparin

98

What do you call a group of inherited disorders marked by increased bleeding times?

A) Anemias
B) Leukemias
C) Hemophilias
D) Polycythemias

Which of the following blood sample tubes can be subject to centrifugation immediately after collection?

A) Clot tubes
B) Thrombin tubes
C) Sodium citrate tubes
D) Serum separator tubes

100

In the modified Allen test, one hand is examined at a time. The hand is elevated, and the patient is asked to clench his/her fist for about 30 seconds. The pressure is applied over the ulnar and the radial arteries to occlude both of them.

Which of the following factors is determined using the modified Allen test?

A) pH

B) Collateral circulation

C) The partial pressure of oxygen

D) The partial pressure of carbon dioxide

101

What is most likely to happen to the blood's pH if the stopper is removed from a blood sample tube?

A) The pH may increase.

B) The pH may decrease.

C) The pH will not change.

D) The pH becomes alkaline.

102

Iontophoretic sweet test or the chloride sweat test is done to detect the amount of chloride and sodium found in sweat.

Which of the following conditions is being screened by the iontophoretic sweet test?

A) Spina bifida

B) Cystic fibrosis

C) Multiple sclerosis

D) Myasthenia gravis

103

Standard Precautions are the basic level infection prevention practices used in the care of all patients, regardless of suspected or confirmed infection status of the patient.

Which of the following is true about standard precautions?

A) They must be used at all times for all patients in all situations.

B) They aim to reduce the risk of transmission of microorganisms from both recognized and unrecognized infection sources in healthcare settings.

C) They include handwashing, personal protective equipment such as gloves, gowns, and masks whenever exposure to patients' body fluids is anticipated.

D) All of the above

104

Phenylketonuria (PKU) test is done to check if a newborn baby has the enzyme needed to use phenylalanine in their body.

Where are samples for PKU testing usually collected?

A) In a micropipette

B) In a collection tube

C) On special filter paper

D) In a micro collection container

105

Glucose is the main source of energy in the body. The ability of a human body to use glucose is measured by the oral glucose tolerance test (OGTT). It is usually done to diagnose prediabetes or diabetes especially in pregnant women.

For a 3-hour OGTT, The first blood draw will be taken upon arrival to the lab. How many additional blood draws does this test involve?

A) 3

B) 4

C) 5

D) None of the above.

106

A mechanical pump that functions to assist cardiac circulation is called the **ventricular assist device (VAD)**. It is usually used to either partially or entirely replace the function of a failing heart.

Which of the following does not belong to VAD?

A) IV

B) CVC

C) PICC

D) EMLA

107

An organism that spreads infection by being a carrier of pathogens from one host to another but does not cause disease to itself is called a **vector**.

Which of the following about vectors is true?

A) Diseases transmitted by vectors are called vector-borne diseases.

B) Mosquito, which transmits the deadly disease Malaria, is the most common vector for human infection.

C) Many vector-borne diseases are zoonotic diseases that can be transmitted directly or indirectly between animals and humans.

D) All of the above

108

It causes the gradual failure of the immune system and slows down the thrive of life-threatening infections and cancers. The human immunodeficiency virus causes it.

Which of the following disease is explained above?

A) AIDS

B) Hepatitis B

C) Gonorrhea

D) Food poisoning

109

There are eight types of herpes viruses that are capable of infecting humans. Varicella-zoster virus (VZV) is one of them.

Which of the following infections is caused by VZV?

A) Malaria

B) Syphilis

C) Hepatitis

D) Chickenpox

110

The National Fire Protection Association (NFPA) diamond is designed to give information about the general hazards of different chemicals.

Which of the following information is not included in the NFPA symbol?

A) Fire

B) Health

C) Chemical stability

D) Protective equipment

111

Which of the following are included in the chain of infection?

A) Opportunism, weakness, immunity, and colonization

B) Intrinsic, extrinsic, internal, and external transmission

C) Active natural, active artificial, passive natural, and passive artificial

D) Germ, agent, reservoir, exit portal, mode of transmission, entry port, and susceptible host

The tube passed through a vein ending up in the vena cava's thoracic portion is the **central venous catheter (CVC)**. It serves as a significant line used to input different medications, nutrients or blood products, and fluids over a long time.

Which of the following is not a type of CVC?

A) Fistula

B) Broviac

C) Groshong

D) Triple lumen

SECTION 5 PROCEDURES

#	Answer	Topic	Subtopic	#	Answer	Topic	Subtopic	#	Answer	Topic	Subtopic	#	Answer	Topic	Subtopic
1	D	TB	S1	29	B	TB	S3	57	B	TB	S1	85	B	TB	S3
2	A	TB	S3	30	B	TB	S1	58	D	TB	S3	86	A	TB	S2
3	C	TB	S2	31	C	TB	S2	59	C	TB	S2	87	C	TB	S2
4	A	TB	S2	32	D	TB	S4	60	B	TB	S2	88	B	TB	S1
5	C	TB	S2	33	C	TB	S4	61	C	TB	S3	89	D	TB	S4
6	C	TB	S2	34	A	TB	S2	62	D	TB	S2	90	A	TB	S3
7	B	TB	S2	35	B	TB	S2	63	B	TB	S1	91	D	TB	S3
8	B	TB	S4	36	D	TB	S2	64	D	TB	S4	92	A	TB	S2
9	C	TB	S2	37	C	TB	S1	65	C	TB	S2	93	C	TB	S4
10	D	TB	S2	38	D	TB	S2	66	B	TB	S3	94	A	TB	S2
11	B	TB	S1	39	D	TB	S2	67	D	TB	S2	95	C	TB	S4
12	C	TB	S2	40	D	TB	S3	68	B	TB	S2	96	A	TB	S1
13	D	TB	S1	41	C	TB	S1	69	C	TB	S1	97	B	TB	S2
14	D	TB	S3	42	B	TB	S3	70	B	TB	S4	98	C	TB	S1
15	A	TB	S3	43	A	TB	S2	71	D	TB	S2	99	C	TB	S4
16	A	TB	S2	44	C	TB	S2	72	B	TB	S2	100	B	TB	S2
17	B	TB	S1	45	D	TB	S1	73	D	TB	S1	101	A	TB	S4
18	A	TB	S3	46	D	TB	S2	74	C	TB	S2	102	B	TB	S2
19	D	TB	S2	47	B	TB	S2	75	C	TB	S1	103	D	TB	S3
20	D	TB	S3	48	C	TB	S3	76	A	TB	S2	104	C	TB	S2
21	B	TB	S3	49	B	TB	S2	77	D	TB	S2	105	A	TB	S2
22	D	TB	S4	50	B	TB	S3	78	D	TB	S2	106	D	TB	S2
23	D	TB	S2	51	A	TB	S1	79	C	TB	S3	107	D	TB	S3
24	B	TB	S4	52	C	TB	S3	80	C	TB	S3	108	A	TB	S3
25	C	TB	S4	53	C	TB	S3	81	C	TB	S2	109	D	TB	S3
26	D	TB	S3	54	D	TB	S3	82	D	TB	S4	110	D	TB	S1
27	B	TB	S3	55	C	TB	S3	83	C	TB	S2	111	D	TB	S3
28	D	TB	S3	56	A	TB	S2	84	C	TB	S2	112	A	TB	S2

Topics & Subtopics

Code	Description	Code	Description
SB1	Care & Safety	SB4	Specimen Transport Handling & Processing
SB2	Collection Procedures	TB	Procedures
SB3	Infection Control		

CONTINUE ▶

TEST DIRECTION

DIRECTIONS

Read the questions carefully and then choose the ONE best answer to each question.

Be sure to allocate your time carefully so you are able to complete the entire test within the testing session. You may go back and review your answers at any time.

You may use any available space in your test booklet for scratch work.

Questions in this booklet are not actual test questions but they are the samples for commonly asked questions.

This test aims to cover all topics which may appear on the actual test. However some topics may not be covered.

Studying this booklet will be preparing you for the actual test. It will not guarantee improving your test score but it will help you pass your exam on the first attempt.

Some useful tips for answering multiple choice questions;

- Start with the questions that you can easily answer.

- Underline the keywords in the question.

- Be sure to read all the choices given.

- Watch for keywords such as NOT, always, only, all, never, completely.

- Do not forget to answer every question.

## 1

A **blood donation** is an essential contribution to save a life for patients with serious medical conditions or improve their health. **Blood donors** are real-life heroes for voluntarily give their blood for transfusion.

Which of the following is the proper way of giving care to a donor after a blood collection?

I. Instruct the donor to sit still and relax for a few minutes.
II. Check the venipuncture site for bleeding and apply further pressure if needed.
III. Tell the donor to instantly sit up so blood can distribute faster in their body.
IV. Request the donor to stand-up right after blood collection so they can take a rest in the waiting area.
V. Offer the donor some refreshments.

A) I, II, V
B) I, II, III, V
C) II, III, IV, V
D) I, II, III, IV, V

## 2

Anticoagulant agents, commonly known as blood thinners, are chemical substances that prevent the coagulation of blood. They extend the time for the specialists to work on the blood for different tests.

Which of the following tests must have a 9:1 ratio of blood to anticoagulant in the collection tube?

A) Protime
B) Electrolytes
C) Blood culture
D) Two-hour PP

3

A **CTAD Tube** can be identified from the color of its stopper, which is light blue. The CTAD Tube is used for the coagulation test.

Which of the following is the reason for the use of a CTAD Tube?

A) To increase clotting time.

B) To inhibit platelet activation.

C) To inhibits alcohol volatization.

D) To inhibit red blood cells from separating.

4

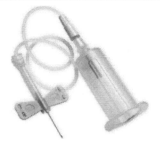

In phlebotomy, a **butterfly needle** is a device used to access a vein to collect blood samples.

Which of the following states why butterfly needles are advantageous to use?

A) Butterflies are less expensive.

B) Butterflies increase the patient's blood flow.

C) Butterflies make drawing problematic veins easier.

D) Butterflies have a greater choice of needle sizes.

5

A **tourniquet** is a device commonly used by phlebotomists to draw blood more efficiently. The device tightens the limbs for the veins to bulge and checks which one is most suitable for venipuncture.

When should you release the tourniquet?

A) Before the needle is removed from the arm

B) Within a minute that it has been placed

C) After blood flow is established

D) All of the above

6

There are different needles to choose from when collecting blood samples, depending on what is needed.

What is the possible largest gauge number of needles?

A) 16 gauge

B) 20 gauge

C) 21 gauge

D) 23 gauge

7

Where should the tourniquet be placed when executing butterfly draw using a hand vein?

A) On the patient's wrist

B) On the patient's arm below the antecubital fossa

C) On the patient's arm above the antecubital fossa

D) A tourniquet is not required for a butterfly draw

8

Clinical laboratories are healthcare facilities that provide a wide range of laboratory procedures to aid physicians in carrying out the diagnosis, treatment, and management of patients.

There are various positions within a clinical laboratory based on a career ladder of academic and technical milestones.

Which of the following laboratory roles is correctly correlated?

A) The laboratory director is usually a board-certified medical doctor, PhD scientist or a medical laboratory scientist.

B) The laboratory director and the laboratory administrator share responsibilities for managing the laboratory.

C) The pathologist is a physician who specializes in diagnosing disease through the use of laboratory tests.

D) All of the above

9

Puncture devices puncture off the skin with a needle or introducer to provide an entry site. There are a variety of disposable skin puncture devices that will ensure a safe procedure when used correctly.

What should be the maximum length of a puncture device used on the heel?

A) 1.00 mm

B) 1.25 mm

C) 1.50 mm

D) 2.00 mm

As a phlebotomy technician, which of the following do you think is the most appropriate action if a patient is not in his room when a stat test is being ordered?

A) You should find the patient.

B) You may postpone the collection.

C) You should wait in the patient's room until he or she returns.

D) You can leave the request at the nurse's station for the nurse to perform the draw.

Collection tubes used to store the blood specimen from the venipuncture procedure includes some features that can be used to identify their content. The most common of these features is the color of the tube's stopper, indicating its content and the specimen that can be placed.

Which of the following tubes contains an anticoagulant that inhibits thrombin?

A) Gray stopper

B) Violet stopper

C) Green stopper

D) Light blue stopper

12

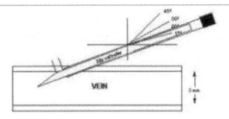

A **rolling vein** is the type of vein that can move quickly upon the insertion of a needle or the IV. The phlebotomist must determine that the vein is not a rolling vein when doing venipuncture.

Which of the following is the step of primary importance to prevent rolling veins?

A) Use 25-gauge needle
B) Tightly apply tourniquet
C) Select the appropriate vein
D) Anchor the vein when inserting the needle

13

When entering a patient's room, which of the following should you do first as the attending phlebotomy technician?

A) You should introduce yourself first.
B) You should identify the patient first.
C) You should put your gloves on first.
D) You should assemble first your equipment

14

Povidone-iodine is an antiseptic used to disinfect the skin before and after surgery to prevent infection.

Which of the following procedures does not require the use of a povidone-iodine solution in the blood collection site?

A) Blood culture collection
B) Blood donation collection
C) Arterial blood gas collection
D) Therapeutic drug monitoring collection

15

What information should be matched with the patient's ID band and the requisition?

A) DOB
B) ID number
C) Patient's name
D) Name of the physician

6

16

Asepsis is the state in which no living disease-causing microorganisms are present. It has been derived from the 19th-century antiseptic techniques that introduced sterilizing surgical tools and the wearing of surgical gloves during operations.

Which of the following is the goal of asepsis?

A) Ensure the maximum use of surgical tools by physical judgment

B) Eliminate infection and not to achieve sterility

C) Contaminate surgery tools and process with pathogens for research purposes

D) All of the above

17

What do we call the small red spots on the skin, possibly due to a tourniquet left placed on a patient for too long?

A) Petechiae

B) Hematoma

C) Nerve damage

D) Occluded radial pulse

18

A sample of arterial blood is collected from an artery to determine arterial blood gases. ABG sampling provides the necessary information on the acid-base balance of a patient's illness.

Which of the following can be the potential complications of arterial blood sampling?

A) Nerve damage

B) Hematoma or excessive bleeding

C) Fainting or a vasovagal response

D) All of the above

19

Which of the following is the phenomenon in which the ratio of formed elements to plasma increases due to the tissue's loss of fluid?

A) Petechiae

B) Hemolysis

C) Hematoma

D) Hemoconcentration

CONTINUE ▶

20

FUO refers to a fever of unknown origin.

Osteomyelitis is an infection in a bone.

Fibrinolysis is the break-down of blood clots.

Bacteremia is the presence of bacteria in the blood.

Septicemia, in other words, blood poisoning, is the presence of pathogens in the circulating bloodstream.

How many of the terms about venipuncture given above are defined correctly?

A) 2

B) 3

C) 4

D) 5

21

A phlebotomist has no other choice but to obtain a specimen from a site with a hematoma.

In which of the following positions should the phlebotomist gather the sample?

A) Distal to the hematoma

B) Proximal to the hematoma

C) In the area of the hematoma

D) All positions are acceptable

22

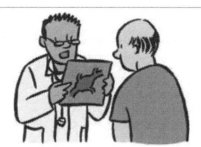

A phlebotomist must successfully perform palpation of a vein to determine that the vein can be used for venipuncture. Complications may start to occur as soon as the needle punctures the wrong vein.

Which of the following does not conform with the correct palpation of vein?

A) Probing by the index finger

B) Determining the vein's depth

C) Detecting the pulse using the thumb

D) Determining the direction of the vein

23

A **winged blood collection set** is a standard medical tool specially used for venipuncture. Sometimes, the set is also used for accessing a vein on the surface of the skin for intravenous injection.

Which of the following is not acceptable while using a winged blood set?

A) Lowering the angle of insertion

B) Using off a 15 mL evacuated tube

C) Threading the needle into the vein

D) Drawing of blood into the syringe used

179

CONTINUE ▶

The **Packed Cell Volume**, or PCV, is a measurement for the proportion of blood. It is expressed in percentage or fraction, in general.

Which of the following is a test that measures packed cell volume?

A) Hct
B) hCG
C) TnT
D) INR

Blood spillage happens when a laboratory sample breaks in the phlebotomy area or during transportation or excessive bleeding during the procedure. Any blood spillage should be decontaminated to prevent the potential transmission of an infectious disease.

Which of the following procedures should not be included in cleaning up the spillage and recording the incident?

1. Wear a pair of sterile gloves.
2. Use tongs or a pan and brush to sweep up as much of the broken glass as possible. Do not pick up pieces with your hands.
3. Discard the broken glass in a regular waste container.
4. Use disposable paper towels to absorb as much of the body fluids as possible.
5. Wipe the area with water and detergent until it is visibly clean.
6. Saturate the area again with sodium hypochlorite 0.5% (10 000 ppm available chlorine).
7. Rinse off the tongs, brush, and pan under running water, and place to dry.
8. Remove gloves and discard them.
9. Wash hands carefully with soap and water, and dry thoroughly with single-use towels.
10. Record the incident in the incident book if a specimen was lost or people were exposed to blood and body fluids.

A) 1 and 3
B) 2 and 6
C) 5 and 8
D) 4 and 9

26

Collecting blood samples is the frequently used method to diagnose and monitor diseases, and the most common way is **venipuncture** which means collecting blood from a vein.

Which of the following requirements is correct for a collection system for blood donation?

A) Furniture and equipment in the blood donation and processing area should be made of absorbent surfaces like fabric rather than vinyl.

B) Containers used to transport supplies and specimens should be cleanable by disinfectants such as sodium hypochlorite bleach solutions.

C) All equipment used to collect blood donations should be annually calibrated, maintained, and serviced, such as blood pressure monitors, scales, blood bag tube sealers, and blood bank refrigerators.

D) All of the above

27

The capillaries in the body are branching blood vessels between the arteries and the veins. The capillaries are much smaller, and they are usually punctured as an alternative if venipuncture cannot be made.

Which of the following is described by "**capillary action**"?

A) The capillaries are pulsing.
B) Blood fills a microhematocrit tube.
C) Venous blood is entering the capillary.
D) Arterial blood is entering the capillary.

28

Before you can donate blood, some criteria should be met, including your overall health, age, and donation frequency. Previous medical issues like infection or scarring also need to be assessed.

Which of the following should be assessed or met before venipuncture for blood donation?

I. Age
II. Height and eyesight
III. Donor's written consent
IV. Weight and blood pressure
V. Fluid restriction to reduce risk of fainting after blood donation

A) I, III, IV
B) I, II, II, IV
C) I, III, IV, V
D) I, II, III, IV, V

29

What should be the angle when a venipuncture needle penetrates the skin?

A) 10° to 15°
B) 15° to 30°
C) 30° to 40°
D) 45° to 60°

30

Fainting refers to sudden loss of consciousness caused by dilation of blood vessels and slow heart rate that decreased blood flow to our brain. During venipuncture, fainting is very common that can be caused by the sight of an injection needle, blood, or when standing up for too long. Doctors medically call it a vasovagal episode since a stimulus in the vagus nerve triggers it.

Which of the following aids is false when someone losses consciousness during blood collection?

A) Keep using ammonia inhalants on the patient until he/she regains consciousness.
B) Lay the patient flat if possible or lower his/her head and arms.
C) Start to loosen the patient's tight clothing if he/she is standing.
D) Press the Emergency Buzzer located at every drawing area to notify the pre-surgery screening nurse.

31

Generally, blood collection tubes have additives in them that act as a clot activator or anticoagulant.

What color/type of tube does not contain any additives?

A) Dark blue
B) Red glass tube
C) Red plastic tube
D) Gold BD HemogardTM

32

Which of the following is a constituent of the media if the tube has green color stoppers?

A) Sodium citrate

B) Sodium heparin

C) Sodium oxalate

D) Sodium phosphate

33

In which laboratory department is special patient identification required?

A) Chemistry department

B) Blood bank department

C) Hematology department

D) Microbiology department

34

When collecting blood, all the equipment must be clean and ready. The phlebotomist must have the proper knowledge to check the requirements and explain the venipuncture process to the blood donors.

Which of the following should a phlebotomist monitor when doing a venipuncture for a blood donor?

A) Sweating or feeling of fainting

B) Development of a hematoma at the injection site

C) Change in blood flow that may indicate the needle has moved in the vein and needs reposition

D) All of the above

35

Harry, a phlebotomist, was assigned to perform venipuncture on a patient, and noticed that the patient has three good veins in the antecubital area.

Which of the following veins should Harry choose as the blood collection site?

A) Basilic vein

B) Brachial vein

C) Cephalic vein

D) Median cubital vein

36

Hematoma or excessive bleeding refers to the irregular collection of blood outside of blood vessels. It can be caused an injury to the blood vessel wall, artery, or vein that prompts blood to drip out of the blood vessel into the surrounding tissues.

Which of the following will prevent hematoma on arterial blood sampling?

A) Tell the patient to relax.

B) Apply pressure immediately after blood is drawn.

C) Insert the needle without puncturing the far side of the vessel.

D) All of the above

37

The tubes with gray stoppers are used for which of the following?

A) Coagulation studies

B) Glucose tolerance test

C) Sedimentation rate test

D) Complete blood count (CBC)

38

Antiseptics are used to prevent the spread of disease-causing microorganisms. They kill and neutralize most of these microorganisms to safe levels.

Which of the following antiseptics is used primarily for routine venipuncture?

A) Iodine

B) Betadine

C) Isopropyl alcohol

D) Liquid salt and detergent

39

A **nursing home** refers to a public or private residential facility providing care to elderly or disabled people who don't necessarily need to be in a hospital but can't be cared for at home.

Which of the following is true when collecting blood in nursing home settings?

A) Identification of patients must be documented and done by an authorized employee of the facility.

B) The identifying individual must accompany the blood/specimen collector to the patient's bedside for proper identification.

C) The nursing home employee must sign an outpatient specimen form after the blood collection.

D) All of the above

40

Lancets are sharp-pointed needles used to make punctures for blood collections. The depth of skin penetration depends on several factors, like skin thickness.

How many millimeters must be the skin penetration depth to obtain blood samples in new-born babies?

A) 2.4 mm or less

B) 2.6 mm or less

C) 2.8 mm or less

D) 3.0 mm or less

41

Needles used for venipuncture are hollow and longer to help ease the process. The thickness of the needle largely depends on some circumstances.

Which of the following are the criteria used for determining the size of the needle?

A) Personal preference

B) The deepness of the vein

C) The test type for the specimen

D) The size and condition of the vein

42

Allen test refers to a procedure used to assess if the blood flow to your hand is normal. It is performed to determine if collateral circulation is present from the ulnar artery if thrombosis occurs in the radial artery.

Which of the following instructions is the proper way to perform an Allen test?

A) Tell the patient to elevate his/her hand and clench his/her fist, but when unable to do, instruct to close the hand tightly.

B) Apply occlusive pressure using your fingers to both the ulnar and radial arteries to obstruct blood flow to the hand.

C) To check if you apply complete occlusive pressure to both arteries, let the patient relax his/her hand, and check whether the palm and fingers have blanched.

D) All of the above

Venipuncture is the medical term used for the puncturing of a patient's vein. It is usually done for drawing off blood or intravenous injection of medicine. **On** the other hand, EMLA is an anesthetic cream with a mixture of 2.5% lidocaine and 2.5% prilocaine.

Which of the following is the specific use of "EMLA"?

A) Topical anesthetic applied to the child's arm before venipuncture.

B) Local anesthesia to numb the skin of the child before venipuncture.

C) The anesthetic medicine is taken by a child an hour before venipuncture.

D) Skincare solution applied to a child's skin to assist in finding the vein of the child.

Osteomyelitis is the clinical term for an infection in the bone or bone marrow that causes inflammation. Staphylococcus bacteria commonly cause this infection and are usually transmitted through the bloodstream or spreading from one tissue to another. On the other hand, **hemolysis** refers to the destruction or breakdown of red blood cells (RBCs), leading to hemoglobin release from RBCs into the blood plasma.

Which of the following scenarios can probably cause osteomyelitis?

A) Spleen traps and destroys healthy red blood cells due to tumors.

B) Bacteria in the bloodstream is deposited in a focal area of the bone.

C) A patient receives a red blood cell transfusion of the wrong blood type.

D) All of the above

CONTINUE ▶

45

Reflux of anticoagulants is the flow of blood from the collection tube back into the needle and then into the patient's vein.

Which of the following can be done to avoid the reflux of anticoagulants?

A) Allow the tube to fill from the bottom up.
B) Remove the last tube from the needle before removing the needle.
C) Remove the last tube from the needle before removing the tourniquet.
D) All of the above

46

During arterial collection, what should be the angle of the needle when inserted into the artery?

A) 30 degrees
B) 45 degrees
C) 70 degrees
D) 90 degrees

47

Needles are a slim, sharp-pointed instrument used in puncturing tissues, stitching up wounds, or passing a ligature through or around a vessel.

In which of the following circumstances should needles be recapped?

A) After the collection of blood gases
B) After gathering a specimen in a syringe
C) After the collection of a sample in the emergency room
D) Used needles must be placed in sharps disposal containers without recapping.

48

A **blood smear** is a test conducted to examine and determine any abnormalities in the blood cells.

Which of the following options is a characteristic of an acceptable blood smear?

A) It is thick and short.
B) It must form the shape of a bullet.
C) It has a feathered, almost square edge.
D) It must cover the whole surface of the slide.

49

An **evacuated tube system** is a piece of equipment usually used in routine venipuncture.

This equipment consists of which of the following materials?

A) Evacuated sample tube, special plastic adapter, and a syringe

B) Winged infusion set, plastic holder, and a double-pointed needle

C) Anticoagulant, special plastic adapter, and a double-pointed needle

D) Evacuated sample tube, plastic adapter, and a double-pointed needle

50

Veins are a vital component of the cardiovascular system. They are the blood vessels that carry deoxygenated blood to the heart.

Which of the following terms may refer to a vein that lacks flexibility and feels hard and cord-like?

A) An artery

B) A collapsed vein

C) A superficial vein

D) A thrombosed vein

51

Arteriospasm refers to spasm or the involuntary contraction of the artery resulting in a decrease of its caliber. This pain is commonly felt under the chest bone or left side of the chest.

Which of the following examples will help to prevent arteriospasm?

A) Expose the patient to colder areas.

B) Explain the procedure and position the person comfortably.

C) Allow the patient to eat more than they can.

D) All of the above

52

A **nerve** refers to one or more bundles of fibers that receive and send messages between the body and the brain. Damage to our nerves can affect our brain's ability to communicate with our muscles and organs.

Which of the following will prevent nerve damage on arterial blood sampling?

A) Allow redirection of the needle.

B) Choose an appropriate sampling site.

C) Do not disclose the procedure to the patient.

D) All of the above

53

What factor is not affected by the patient's condition when having laboratory tests?

A) Albumin
B) Enzymes
C) Cholesterol
D) Blood alcohol

54

Sharie is a nurse in a hospital. She collected a blood sample from a patient and placed it in a light blue-stoppered tube.

What test will be performed if the sample is placed in a light blue-stoppered tube?

A) Toxicology
B) Coagulation
C) Glucose tolerance
D) Sedimentation rate

CONTINUE ▶

55

Inappropriate handling and collection of arterial blood specimens can lead to incorrect results. It is the primary responsibility of a phlebotomist to follow the correct protocols in doing arterial blood sampling.

Which of the following will not cause an inaccurate blood result?

A) Presence of air in the sample
B) Delay in specimen transportation
C) Collection of arterial rather than venous blood
D) Improper quantity of heparin in the syringe or improper mixing after blood is drawn.

56

Which of the following is not true when an artery is accidentally stuck during blood collection?

A) The blood will be bright red.
B) The sample should be discarded.
C) The blood may spurt or pulse into the tube.
D) Pressure should be applied for 5 minutes.

57

Arterial blood gas (ABG) sampling by direct vascular puncture is often practiced in the hospital setting. Healthcare personnel should wear gloves and eye protection for the duration of the ABG.

Among the choices given, which one is not an error that often occurs during ABG sampling?

A) Air bubbles in the syringe
B) Use of the anticoagulant EDTA
C) Use of a plastic syringe that is gas-impermeable
D) Delivery of an un-iced sample to the lab 15 minutes after collection

58

If you have an obese patient, what vein is the only one that can be palpated?

A) Iliac vein
B) Basilic vein
C) Median vein
D) Cephalic vein

## 59

Venipuncture is the most preferred blood sampling method for pediatric and neonatal patients since it causes less pain than heel-pricks. Pediatric patients are aged 21 or younger, while neonatal patients are less than 28 days old.

Which of the following is TRUE about pediatric and neonatal blood sampling?

A) Use a syringe with a barrel volume of 1 –5 ml.

B) Use a winged steel needle, preferably 23 gauge with an extension tube.

C) Finger-prick or a heel-prick method will depend on the age and weight of the child.

D) All of the above

## 60

Reference laboratory refers to a large independent laboratory that receives a specimen from another laboratory or healthcare facility that performs one or more tests on the given specimen.

Which of the following is **true** about the benefits of sending specimens to a reference laboratory?

A) Lower cost per test due to high volume of tests

B) Provide more specialized analysis of patient specimen

C) More time-efficient logging or documenting receipt of a specimen

D) All of the above

## 61

Pediatricians are legally allowed to draw blood and collect samples from a child patient. Drawing blood and saliva collection are one of the most common procedures for determining a child's illness.

Which of the following pediatric tools is required to collect blood for a pediatric venipuncture?

A) Emergency singlets

B) Winged infusion set

C) Plastic capillary tubes

D) Plastic capillary/vein sealer

## 62

Ethylenediaminetetraacetic acid (EDTA) is a compound that has various medical uses, such as an anticoagulant.

How is coagulation in the blood tubes prevented by EDTA?

A) By inhibiting glycolysis

B) By binding with calcium

C) By inactivating thrombin

D) By inactivating thromboplastin

CONTINUE ▶

63

- First and last name
- Patient ID
- Date of birth
- Gender
- Specimen type
- Tests required
- Sample date and time
- Relevant clinical details
- Name of clinician requesting blood

How many of the information given above must a blood request form contain?

A) 6
B) 7
C) 8
D) 9

64

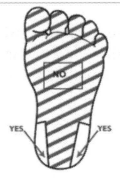

Newborn infants are recognized to have small and fragile veins. Dermal punctures are used to obtain blood from them to simplify the acquisition and avoid complications of doing a venipuncture.

Which of the following are the areas where dermal punctures can be made to a newborn infant?

A) Back of the hand
B) Medial plantar areas of the heel
C) Lateral plantar areas of the heel
D) Both B and C

65

Who among the patients given below has the greatest advantage when using the syringe method in blood collection?

A) Patients who are obese
B) Patients who are very young
C) Patients who have large veins
D) Patients who have fragile or small veins

66

Doctors have ordered four various tests at the same time on different inpatients. Jeremy, a phlebotomist, was the only one on duty. The tests he needed to perform were as follows: ASAP CBC in Oncology, STAT electrolytes in the ER, time blood cultures in the ICU, and hemoglobin in labor and delivery.

Which of the following tests should he do first?

A) ASAP CBC in Oncology
B) STAT electrolytes in the ER
C) Time blood cultures in the ICU
D) Hemoglobin in labor and delivery

67

A **requisition** is an act of formally requiring or calling upon someone to act. In the medical profession, doctors complete a requisition form when requesting lab tests.

Among the actions given below, which one is not a purpose of requisition?

A) Identifying the patient
B) Filing insurance claims
C) Determining the specimens to be collected
D) Allowing the equipment necessary for the collection to be gathered

68

The blood collection system is **"closed"** when the drawn blood passes directly into the tube with no exposure to the environment or healthcare professionals.

Which of the following is not included in the World Health Organization (**WHO**) guidelines on drawing blood in a closed collection system?

A) There must be a sterile blood collection bag containing an anticoagulant and an integrally attached tube and needle.
B) Diversion pouches are sometimes included to minimize contamination from skin flora and the skin core.
C) A reusable lancet is appropriate when gathering blood for hemoglobin testing with a capillary stick.
D) None of the above

69

Which of the following should be done to the tubes for blood collection containing an anticoagulant?

A) The tubes must be inverted repeatedly and gently after blood collection.

B) The tubes must be shaken aggressively after blood collection.

C) The tubes must be allowed to sit for 30 minutes before centrifugation.

D) The tubes must be centrifuged immediately after blood collection.

70

A **hypodermic needle** refers to a hollow needle commonly used with a syringe to inject or extract substances into and from the body.

How many of the features below are the advantages of hypodermic single-use needle and syringe?

I. Least expensive
II. Widely available
III. Does not require special training
IV. Comes in a wide range of needle lengths and gauges
V. Can be used for drawing blood in the pediatric population
VI. For a patient with small or difficult veins, drawing blood can be easier than an evacuated tube system.
VII. If heparinized, hypodermic single-use needle and syringe can be used for arterial blood drawing.

A) 4
B) 5
C) 6
D) 7

71

Venipuncture is a common procedure that is used to draw and collect blood or infuse medicine for a patient. The patient's vein is punctured by a sterile syringe.

Which of the following blood test is recommended for venipuncture?

A) Hematocrit
B) Hemoglobin
C) Blood culture
D) Timed glucose

72

Which of the following statements is correct about gauge needle numbers?

A) The lumen diameter is larger if the gauge number is smaller.
B) The lumen diameter is smaller if the gauge number is smaller.
C) The needle is longer if the gauge number is smaller.
D) The needle is shorter if the gauge number is smaller.

73

Fainting or a vasovagal response refers to the sudden loss of consciousness when something interrupts our brain, like decreased blood flow.

Which of the following will prevent fainting on arterial blood sampling?

A) Tell the patient to drink lots of fluids rich in sugar.
B) Instruct the patient to bend his/her knee and lower head.
C) Ensure that the patient is lying down on their back with feet elevated before beginning the blood draw.
D) All of the above

## 74

Patient immobilization is vital to the safety and success of pediatric and neonatal blood sampling. A phlebotomist must know how to effectively draw blood as younger children can only understand feeling more than needs which resistance will occur.

Which of the following techniques must be implemented during pediatric and neonatal blood sampling?

I. Tell the parent to tighten the child's wrist to restrict blood flow.

II. Assign one phlebotomist as technician and another phlebotomist or a parent to immobilize the child.

III. Put cold compressed on the area of puncture to help contract the blood vessels.

IV. Use a transilluminator or pocket pen light to display the dorsal hand veins and the antecubital fossa's veins.

V. Stretch immobilizer's arm across the table and place the child on the back with head on top of the outstretched arm.

VI. Keep the child warm to increase the blood flow rate by removing a few of the child's clothes.

A) I, II, III

B) II, IV, V, VI

C) II, III, IV, V

D) I, II, III , V, VI

Implied consent is an unwritten consent that can be accepted by bodily actions. Such consent is legal but with limitations such as the place, the gesture, and the act to be committed.

Which of the following is required for an implied consent of an adult for venipuncture?

A) Patient's signature

B) Presence of a witness

C) Patient extending his/her arm

D) Presence of the physician or nurse

Which of the following prohibits the recollection of specimen?

A) Using the wrong antiseptic
B) Accidental puncture of an artery
C) Incomplete drying of the antiseptic
D) Contamination by powder from gloves

Needles are one of the most valuable tools used when collecting blood samples from patients.

Color-coding of needles indicate which of the following details?

A) Gauge
B) Length
C) Manufacturer
D) Angle of the bevel

A **venipuncture** is done to collect blood specimens for the specific tests that the physician requires on the patient. The specimen is collected using vacuum tubes.

Which of the following is not an apparatus for a routine venipuncture?

A) EST Tubes
B) Tourniquet
C) Safety needles
D) Iodine cotton swab

When planning for a blood donation drive, one of the main priorities is choosing the location. As donors need to either sit or lie down during blood collection, premises should be of sufficient size.

Which of the following conditions should be met in considering the location for blood donation?

I. Floors should be carpeted.
II. Premises should have separate clean and dirty areas, clean running water, and surfaces cleanable by disinfectants for efficient operations.
III. There must be a waiting area inside the collection site to contain respiratory pathogens for workers.
IV. All fixed and mobile blood donation sites should meet defined standards of environmental safety.
V. An organized donation sites avoid errors during the blood donation process to ensure everyone's safety.

A) I, IV, V
B) I, III, V
C) II, IV, V
D)   I, II, III, IV, V

Blood can no longer flow freely through a **collapsed vein**.

Which of the following is the main cause of collapsed veins?

A) The plunger is being pulled too quickly.
B) There is too much vacuum asserted on the vessel.
C) The needle used for collection is too large for the vein.
D) All of the above.

81

For ABG tests, the oxygen setting is crucial for analyzing different gases on the patient's blood. A phlebotomist is requested to draw a specimen while the patient is breathing room air.

If the patient is still on a ventilator during the time for specimen collection, which of the following should the phlebotomist do?

A) Return after 12 hours to collect the specimen.

B) Consult with the patient's nurse to determine what to do.

C) Directly draw the specimen, then add remarks for the event.

D) Remove the ventilator away from the patient, then draw the blood specimen.

82

The type of needle used for venipuncture depends on the tests that the specimen collected will undergo. Some other things that are considered for the kind of needle to be used include the patient's condition and age.

Which of the following is the needle with the smallest diameter?

A) 18-gauge needle

B) 20-gauge needle

C) 21-gauge needle

D) 23-gauge needle

83

How far should be the tourniquet from the venipuncture site when placing it?

A) 1 to 2 inches

B) 2 to 3 inches

C) 3 to 4 inches

D) 4 to 5 inches

84

A **winged infusion set** or butterfly set is a specialized device used for venipuncture. This collection set usually targets superficial veins for phlebotomy or intravenous injection.

Which of the following is the winged blood collection set primarily used for?

A) Stable veins

B) Sturdy veins

C) Finger and heel sticks

D) Difficult and hand veins

## 85

I. A sample of arterial blood is collected from an artery.
II. Arterial blood is the deoxygenated blood in the circulatory system.
III. A sample of arterial blood is collected to determine arterial blood gases.
IV. Arterial blood is dark red in color but looks purple through the translucent skin.

How many of the explanations above about arterial blood sample collection is correct?

A) 1
B) 2
C) 3
D) 4

## 86

What type of gauge needle is used for blood collection from donors for blood banks that will eventually be used for blood transfusions?

A) 16 gauge needle
B) 20 gauge needle
C) 25 gauge needle
D) 23 gauge needle

Auto-disable (AD) syringes are syringes that automatically become disabled after a single-use. It contributes to safety mainly in developing countries where the reuse of standard disposable syringes and resale of used medical equipment is common. However, AD syringes are designed for injection and are not appropriate for phlebotomy.

How many of the following features below are the disadvantages of auto-disable (AD) syringes?

I. Requires additional training
II. Designed to prevent reuse
III. Does not offer needle-stick prevention
IV. Air in the syringe can affect test results
V. Difficult to draw large or multiple blood samples
VI. Requires blood transfer that creates a risk of needle-stick injuries
VII. During probing, a safety mechanism can be activated, requiring new venepuncture.

A) 4
B) 5
C) 6
D) 7

The phlebotomist must avoid introducing further complications to the patient if a draw fails to obtain a blood specimen.

Which of the following must have happened after a phlebotomist senses a slight vibration from the needle after failing to draw blood?

A) The vein became narrow.
B) The vein is twisted and swollen.
C) The needle is up against a valve.
D) The vein is deeper than it shows.

89

If a blood sample is placed in a gray-stoppered tube, what test will it most likely undergo?

A) Stat chemistry

B) Stat potassium

C) Fasting Blood Sugar (FBS)

D) Complete Blood Count (CBC)

90

Sheyla makes an error in reporting her patient's blood test results.

Which of the following type(s) of variable occurs in this case?

A) Preexamination variable; processes that occur before testing the sample

B) Examination variable; processes that occur during the testing of the specimens

C) Post examination variable; processes that affect reporting an interpretation of test results

D) All of the above

91

A blood sample is obtained from a patient. It is placed in a lavender-stoppered tube.

What is the test to be performed on the blood sample?

A) Stat chemistry

B) Stat potassium

C) Fasting Blood Sugar (FBS)

D) Complete Blood Count (CBC)

A **modified Allen test** is a procedure to assess the ulnar artery's integrity before a patient undergoes a radial artery sample or puncture.

There are two results for the modified Allen test: positive and negative. **Positive** results refer to the hand's normal flushing and indicate that the ulnar artery has good blood flow. It is determined to be positive if the hand flushes within 5–15 seconds. If it does not within 5-15 seconds, then the result is negative. A **negative** modified Allen test means that ulnar circulation is inadequate or nonexistent, indicating that the radial artery supplying arterial blood to that hand should not be punctured.

What will be the result of the modified Allen tests of Patients Emma and Lilly in the scenario given below?

Emma's hand flushed at 2.2 seconds, while Lilly's hand flushed at 15.0 seconds.

A) Emma - Positive, Lilly - Positive
B) Emma - Positive, Lilly - Negative
C) Emma - Negative, Lilly - Positive
D) Emma - Negative, Lilly - Negative

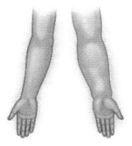

The swelling of the skin may cause a delay in doing venipuncture. The phlebotomist will have to examine the patient and ask the physician if they can draw blood.

Which of the following conditions shows the symptom of a swollen arm with excess fluids?

A) Edema
B) Syncope
C) Hematoma
D) Thrombosed

CONTINUE ▶

94

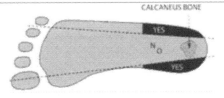

CALCANEUS BONE

Capillary puncture for children and adults can differ mainly due to their tolerance and delicateness. A capillary puncture on the heel is recommended for infants.

Which of the following is the least hazardous area of an infant's foot for a capillary puncture?

A) In the center of the heel
B) Near the toes of the child
C) Lateral plantar heel surface
D) In the back foot part of the heel

95

A phlebotomist is asked to collect a blood specimen from a patient. The patient has no known allergy to antiseptics, according to the tests.

Which of the following substances should be mainly used to clean the site of venipuncture?

A) Povidone-iodine
B) Hydrogen peroxide
C) 70% Isopropyl alcohol
D) Antibacterial soap and water

96

Which of the following is the correct definition of lymphostasis?

A) Lymphostasis is the destruction of blood cells.
B) Lymphostasis is the lack of lymph fluid movement.
C) Lymphostasis is the changing of the ratio of elements in the blood.
D) Lymphostasis is the flow of blood from the collection tube back into the needle and the patient's veins.

97

What condition can cause harm to the patient when drawing blood or change the quality of a specimen?

A) Hematomas
B) Mastectomies
C) Edematous tissue
D) All of the above

CONTINUE ▶

98

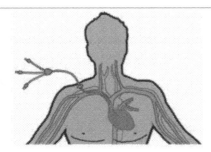

Central Venous Access Devices (CVADs) are medical devices inserted into the body to apply fluid medication. The device is inserted into a vein for easy administration.

Which of the following is attached to CVADs for the collection of blood in evacuated tubes?

A) Luer-Lok to the catheter line
B) 25-gauge needle to the collection syringe
C) Evacuated tube holder to the catheter line
D) Blood transfer device to the collection syringe

99

How many times is a needle allowed to be used before it is discarded?

A) 1
B) 2
C) 3
D) No limit

100

The blood in the human body carries the gases inhaled from the lungs to the system's different parts. An excessive amount or too low off the amount of these gases can be harmful to the body.

Which of the following is a commonly measured ABG parameter?

A) pH
B) Oxygen Saturation
C) PaCO2; The partial pressure of carbon dioxide
D) All of the above

101

Blood fractionation refers to the separation of a blood sample into its parts, which are the red blood cells, white blood cells, and plasma. Each component is placed in separate tubes and subjected to analysis.

Which of the following equipment is used for blood fractionation?

A) Autoclave
B) Centrifuge
C) Hemocytometer
D) UV-Vis Spectrophotometer

102

The blood collection outside the blood vessels due to disease or trauma during surgery or injury is called **a hematoma**. Most hematomas resolve over time as the blood debris is removed and the body's repair mechanisms repair the blood vessel wall.

Which of the following can cause a hematoma?

A) The needle is withdrawn too quickly.

B) The tourniquet is removed after removing the needle.

C) The needle is withdrawn before removing the last tube.

D) The tourniquet is removed before removing the needle.

103

Sodium polyanetholesulfonate (SPS) is an anticoagulant that functions as an inhibitor of antimicrobial systems in the blood. It is commonly used in culture media of blood samples, which helps recover microorganisms in the blood samples by slowing down phagocytes' actions, complements, and certain antibiotics.

What is the purpose of the tubes containing SPS anticoagulant?

A) HLA studies

B) Antibody screen

C) Nutritional analysis

D) Blood culture analysis

104

The major blood vessel that can be found in the upper arms is the **brachial artery**. It is also the continuation of the axillary artery.

What is the vein lying close to the brachial artery?

A) Iliac vein

B) Basilic vein

C) Cephalic vein

D) Median cubital

105

Povidone-iodine (PVP-I), also known as iodopovidine, is used for disinfection before and after surgery.

For which of the following PVP-I is not suggested?

A) Blood cultures

B) Blood gas draws

C) Dermal punctures

D) Blood alcohol draw

106

A phlebotomist determines that an inpatient is not wearing an ID band.

Which of the following is the most appropriate action if venipuncture is to be performed on the patient?

A) The physician should be notified.
B) The venipuncture should not be performed.
C) The patient should be identified by asking his/her name before executing venipuncture.
D) The patient's nurse should be asked to attach a new ID band to the inpatient before doing venipuncture.

107

Venipuncture is referred to as collecting blood samples from a vein that is subject to blood analysis.

Which of the following needles is used for venipuncture?

A) 16 gauge needle
B) 20 gauge needle
C) 25 gauge needle
D) 23 gauge needle

108

A **tourniquet** is a device used for constriction or compression to control arterial and venous circulation to its limit at a certain period.

While performing venipuncture, when should a tourniquet be removed from the arm?

A) As the needle is withdrawn
B) After the needle is withdrawn
C) Before the needle is withdrawn
D) The tourniquet should not be removed

109

An **antiseptic** is a chemical substance that stops or slows down the growth of microorganisms on the body's surface to reduce the possibility of infection, sepsis, or putrefaction.

Which of the following is the most common antiseptic used in routine venipuncture?

A) Bleach
B) Isopropyl alcohol
C) Chlorhexidine gluconate
D) Povidone-iodine solution

110

Coagulation or blood clotting is a significant process usually done by platelets preventing too much bleeding in case of abrasions.

How long would it take for the platelets to complete the coagulation?

A) 10 to 20 minutes

B) 25 to 45 minutes

C) 30 to 60 minutes

D) 30 to 40 minutes

111

Anticoagulants are chemical substances that prevent blood coagulation, resulting in a long time of completion of blood clotting.

Which of the following chemical substances does not belong to anticoagulants?

A) EDTA

B) Sodium citrate

C) Thixotropic gel

D) Sodium heparin

112

Hemolysis involves the disintegration of red blood cells resulting in the release of their cytoplasm into the blood plasma, which can happen either *in vivo* or *in vitro*.

When can hemolysis occur?

A) When the tubes are vigorously mixed

B) When the needle used is larger than 23 gauge

C) When the blood is drawn too slowly into the syringe

D) When the blood is allowed to run down the side of a tube when using a syringe to fill it

SECTION 6 VENIPUNCTURE

#	Answer	Topic	Subtopic	#	Answer	Topic	Subtopic	#	Answer	Topic	Subtopic	#	Answer	Topic	Subtopic
1	A	TC	S2	29	B	TC	S1	57	C	TC	S1	85	B	TC	S1
2	A	TC	S1	30	A	TC	S2	58	D	TC	S1	86	A	TC	S3
3	B	TC	S1	31	B	TC	S3	59	D	TC	S3	87	C	TC	S3
4	C	TC	S3	32	B	TC	S3	60	D	TC	S1	88	C	TC	S2
5	D	TC	S1	33	B	TC	S2	61	B	TC	S3	89	C	TC	S3
6	A	TC	S3	34	D	TC	S3	62	B	TC	S3	90	C	TC	S2
7	A	TC	S2	35	D	TC	S1	63	D	TC	S1	91	D	TC	S3
8	D	TC	S1	36	D	TC	S2	64	D	TC	S1	92	C	TC	S1
9	D	TC	S3	37	B	TC	S3	65	D	TC	S3	93	A	TC	S2
10	A	TC	S2	38	C	TC	S3	66	B	TC	S1	94	C	TC	S3
11	C	TC	S3	39	D	TC	S1	67	B	TC	S1	95	C	TC	S1
12	D	TC	S1	40	A	TC	S3	68	C	TC	S1	96	B	TC	S2
13	B	TC	S1	41	D	TC	S1	69	A	TC	S3	97	D	TC	S2
14	D	TC	S2	42	D	TC	S1	70	D	TC	S3	98	C	TC	S1
15	B	TC	S1	43	A	TC	S1	71	C	TC	S1	99	A	TC	S3
16	B	TC	S1	44	B	TC	S2	72	A	TC	S3	100	D	TC	S1
17	A	TC	S1	45	D	TC	S2	73	C	TC	S2	101	B	TC	S3
18	D	TC	S2	46	B	TC	S1	74	B	TC	S1	102	B	TC	S1
19	D	TC	S1	47	D	TC	S1	75	C	TC	S1	103	D	TC	S3
20	D	TC	S1	48	C	TC	S1	76	B	TC	S2	104	B	TC	S1
21	A	TC	S2	49	D	TC	S3	77	A	TC	S3	105	C	TC	S2
22	C	TC	S1	50	D	TC	S2	78	D	TC	S3	106	C	TC	S1
23	B	TC	S2	51	B	TC	S2	79	C	TC	S3	107	B	TC	S3
24	A	TC	S1	52	B	TC	S2	80	D	TC	S2	108	C	TC	S1
25	A	TC	S2	53	D	TC	S2	81	B	TC	S1	109	B	TC	S3
26	B	TC	S3	54	B	TC	S3	82	D	TC	S3	110	C	TC	S3
27	B	TC	S1	55	C	TC	S1	83	C	TC	S1	111	C	TC	S3
28	A	TC	S3	56	B	TC	S2	84	D	TC	S3	112	A	TC	S2

Topics & Subtopics

Code	Description	Code	Description
SC1	Routine Venipuncture	SC3	Venipuncture Equipment
SC2	Venipuncture Complications	TC	Venipuncture

CONTINUE ▶

TEST DIRECTION

Read the questions carefully and then choose the ONE best answer to each question.

Be sure to allocate your time carefully so you are able to complete the entire test within the testing session. You may go back and review your answers at any time.

You may use any available space in your test booklet for scratch work.

Questions in this booklet are not actual test questions but they are the samples for commonly asked questions.

This test aims to cover all topics which may appear on the actual test. However some topics may not be covered.

Studying this booklet will be preparing you for the actual test. It will not guarantee improving your test score but it will help you pass your exam on the first attempt.

Some useful tips for answering multiple choice questions;

- Start with the questions that you can easily answer.

- Underline the keywords in the question.

- Be sure to read all the choices given.

- Watch for keywords such as NOT, always, only, all, never, completely.

- Do not forget to answer every question.

CONTINUE ▶

1

Which of the following refers to a set of policies and procedures designed to ensure the delivery of consistently high-quality patient care and specimen analysis?

A) Quality control
B) Quality assurance
C) Quality phlebotomy
D) Total quality management

2

The ability to communicate is an essential skill for the phlebotomist.

Which of the following must be avoided while having verbal communication with a patient?

A) Excessive talking
B) Slang or "street" talk
C) Inappropriate terms such as "honey" or "sweetie."
D) All of the above

3

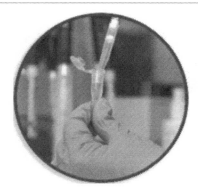

A **specimen** is a small sample that is intended to represent the whole portion for testing with similarity in kind and quality.

Which of the following refers to the phase of collecting and handling specimens?

A) Interphase
B) Metaphase
C) Analytical phase
D) Pre-examination phase

4

For which of the following patients can a legally responsible person give consent?

A) Patients in shock or trauma
B) Patients under the influence of alcohol
C) Patients who are mentally incompetent
D) All of the above

CONTINUE ▶

5

A **laboratory** refers to a facility that conducts scientific and clinical research, product formulation, and reading measurements.

Which of the following US federal agencies handles the regulation of accuracy and quality in laboratories?

A) IRS
B) CMS
C) FCC
D) CLIA

6

Due to modernization, theft does include not only physical objects but also electronic ones. The information placed on a storage device may not seem as secure as you see it.

Which of the following is the law that established national standards for the electronic exchange of protected health information?

A) PHS
B) CLSI
C) OSHA
D) HIPAA

7

How long (approximately) can an infant heel -warming device be applied?

A) 30 seconds
B) 1 to 2 minutes
C) 3 to 5 minutes
D) 8 to 10 minutes

8

What hormone is responsible for the production of glucose by breaking down stored glycogen in the liver?

A) Insulin
B) Glucagon
C) Thymosin
D) Calcitonin

9

A **tort** refers to an act that results in injury or harm to a person and describes as a civil wrong which courts impose liability.

Mia got scheduled for her blood testing. The phlebotomist told her to stay still during blood collection, or else; she will be restrained.

Which of the following torts is involved in the situation?

A) Assault
B) Restriction
C) Malpractice
D) Exploitation

10

In the military, time is spoken differently as compared to how civilians usually read them. This kind of time reading simplifies the need to say the AM/PM partition of the day.

Which of the following is the military equivalent of 10:16 AM?

A) 116
B) 1016
C) 11016
D) 110106

11

A patient that undergoes treatment will be more willing after the experts earn his trust.

Which of the following is a good way for a phlebotomist to earn a patient's trust?

A) Convey sincerity
B) Dress in proper attire
C) Portray your medical expertise
D) All of the above

12

The **cardiovascular system** is the organ system that permits blood circulation. The blood carries essential nutrients and other substances delivered to the different body cells to provide nourishment, maintain body temperature, and fight infections.

How long does it take for the blood to circulate in the body?

A) 30 seconds
B) 45 seconds
C) 60 seconds
D) 75 seconds

13

An institution that offers services to the public is determined by the scope of operations, the type of patients accepted, and the capability of care that they can give.

Which of the following is an institution that provides inpatient services?

A) Clinic
B) Nursery
C) Hospital
D) Research center

14

A phlebotomist is discussing a patient's condition in a public place.

Which of the following can the phlebotomist be accused of?

A) Assault
B) Battery
C) Slander
D) Breach of Confidentiality

15

Drugs are regulated even in hospitals. The intake of all kinds of drugs is given by the recommendation of the attending physician of a patient.

Which of the following department in the hospital prepares and dispenses drugs?

A) Pharmacy
B) Cenral supply
C) Nurse's station
D) Emergency stations

16

Which service of a hospital determines the causes of illness or injury?

A) Support services
B) Diagnostic services
C) Therapeutic services
D) Informational services

17

Most hospitals have their own "clinical" laboratories to perform a wide range of medical tests.

Which of the following clinical studies is not defined correctly?

A) Hematology is the study of human body tissues and cells.

B) Serology is the identification of antibodies in the blood's serum.

C) Toxicology is the study of the adverse effects of chemicals on living organisms.

D) Urinalysis is the physical, chemical, and microscopic examination of urine to discover signs of common diseases and other metabolic problems.

18

Medical malpractice is a legal cause of action. It occurs when a health care professional deviates from standards in their profession and causes injury to a patient.

Which of the following can put a phlebotomist in danger of a malpractice suit?

A) Causing nerve damage to the patient's arm by performing a venipuncture incorrectly.

B) Giving rise to a loss of function to the patient's arm by performing an unauthorized arterial puncture.

C) Resulting in an infected patient not following Occupational Safety and Health Administration (OSHA) standard precautions.

D) All of the above.

19

Viruses, bacteria, and other microorganisms that cause disease are called pathogens. Healthcare workers use the **aseptic technique** to protect patients from pathogens during medical procedures.

Which of the following techniques protect the patient from the transfer of pathogens in a healthcare setting?

A) Using sterile barriers such as gloves, gowns, and masks

B) Cleansing and bacteria-killing preparations to the patient's skin before doing a procedure

C) Maintaining a sterile environment by keeping doors closed and letting only necessary health personnel during the procedures.

D) All of the above

20

Blood in the urine usually indicates an underlying illness such as cancer, kidney stones, and urinary tract infection.

Which of the following terms is the medical term used to refer to blood in the urine?

A) Hematuria

B) Hematoma

C) Hematocrit

D) Hemoglobin

21

Phlebotomy is an ancient practice having roots in Roman and Greek cultures.

Which of the following about the history of bloodletting is true?

A) During the Roman Empire, Galen, a Greek physician, linked organs with blood vessels according to the organ's "supposed" drainage path.

B) According to Galen, the amount of blood to be removed from a patient can be determined by the patient's age, the patient's constitution, the patient's sickness, the weather, the place, and the season.

C) Hippocrates claimed that menstruation purges women of their bad moods. Bloodletting was used to rid the body of evil spirits and treat nearly every disease.

D) All of the above

22

Which of the following body organs is referred to by the prefix hepato-?

A) Liver

B) Blood

C) Heart

D) Kidney

23

A risk manager must determine the areas where the risk can be higher than the usual. She must control the risk within allowable limits or as low as possible, given the resources and circumstances that can be used.

Which of the following does a delta check refer to?

A) Checking the wristband with the requisition

B) Reporting new infection control precautions

C) Documenting all of the results of the QC checks

D) Comparing current test results with the previous one

24

To define a medical word, which of the following should you identify first?

A) Prefix

B) Suffix

C) Word root

D) Combining form

25

Which of the following substances increases when a person cries?

A) Bilirubin

B) Creatinine

C) Platelet count

D) White blood cell count

26

Which of the following refers to an unexpected occurrence involving death or serious physical or psychological injury?

A) Sentinel event

B) Clinical negligence

C) Medication incident

D) Healthcare malpractice

27

The anatomic plane is an imaginary flat surface that divides parts of the body or an organ into the front, back, right, left, upper, and lower sections.

Which of the following is true about the anatomic planes?

A) The frontal plane divides the body into the anterior and posterior portions.
B) The midsagittal plane divides the body vertically into equal right and left portions.
C) The transverse plane divides the body horizontally into superior and inferior portions.
D) All of the above.

28

What does the prefix pulmon- usually refer to?

A) Liver
B) Lung
C) Colon
D) Heart

29

It is a waxy substance found in the blood which is used to make hormones. High levels of it may lead to heart attack, stroke, or other health problems.

Which of the following is defined above?

A) Heparin
B) Albumin
C) Cholesterol
D) Fibrinogen

30

Policies and procedures (P&P) are comprehensive guidelines to communicate to employees the organization's desired outcomes. P&P are the first things a hospital should establish to operate effectively.

Which of the following hospital services sets the policies and procedural activities and runs the hospital?

A) Support services
B) Therapeutic services
C) Administrative services
D) Informational services

31

Which of the following does ABG mean?

A) Arterial Blood Gas
B) Activated Blood Gain
C) Analysed Blood Group
D) Authorized Bleeding Guide

32

If a child has to be held back for a needle-stick, which of the following actions must a phlebotomist do?

A) Ask the parents to assist.
B) Secure the child's arm down.
C) Tell the parents to leave the room.
D) Call an assistant to hold the child down.

33

HIV-AIDS is a viral disease that spreads through sexual interaction with an infected individual. This disease mainly attacks the immune system.

Which of the following about the consent for HIV Testing is true?

A) It requires written consent.
B) It must adhere to state laws.
C) It must be done on an opt-in basis.
D) It must be done on an opt-out basis.

34

Phlebotomists collect different samples for different tests.

Which of the following is true about the sample collection?

A) Cells for DNA analysis may be obtained from a buccal swab.
B) Saliva samples can be used to test for HIV antibodies and hormone levels.
C) Hair samples can detect chronic use of drugs, alcohol, heavy metals, and poisons.
D) All of the above.

35

A healthcare professional must wear proper attire whenever conducting a medical procedure. Maintaining a professional appearance is part of the job.

Which of the following is not part of communicating a professional appearance?

A) Clean cut nails

B) Long hair pulled back

C) Strong smell of alcohol

D) A white, neat, and clean laboratory gown

36

Outpatient (ambulatory) care is any service you receive without being admitted to a hospital or for a visit shorter than 24 hours. When you go to the emergency room, you receive outpatient care until the medical team decides and formally admits you to the hospital. After being officially registered as an inpatient, your care continues on an inpatient basis. Today, lots of procedures don't require overnight stays anymore, thanks to medical technology advances.

Which of the following about outpatient care is true?

A) Some outpatient services are emergency room care, X-rays, minor surgeries, some cancer treatments, and routine physicals.

B) Outpatient procedures generally cost less than comparable inpatient procedures, and patients can recover in the comfort of their own homes.

C) Patients receiving outpatient care don't need to spend a night in a hospital. It may be delivered in many settings, such as your home, a physician's office, or some hospital departments.

D) All of the above

37

You observed that your patient's face is grimacing.

Which of the following is your patient trying to communicate with you nonverbally?

A) Pain
B) Fear
C) Hatred
D) Anxiety

38

Which type of law is created by the administrative agencies such as the Occupational Safety and Health Administration (OSHA)?

A) Case law
B) Federal law
C) Statutory law
D) Administrative law

39

Which of the following is the best time to collect fasting specimens?

A) 24 hours after the fast
B) 2 hours after waking up
C) 8 to 12 hours after eating
D) Any time after midnight

40

NPO is a medical instruction that originates in Latin "Nil per os." There are variations of this instruction, but technically they mean the same thing.

Which of the following does NPO mean?

A) Nothing by mouth
B) New patient ordinances
C) Avoid intake of dark food
D) Nutritionally imbalanced individual

41

The CK blood test is a test that measures the amount of the CK enzyme present in the blood. High CK enzyme levels may indicate a possible disease or damage in the brain, heart, or skeletal muscles.

The abbreviation CK stands for which of the following terms?

A) Citrate Kinase
B) Calcium Kinase
C) Creatine Kinase
D) Cytosine Kinase

42

Which of the following variables does a phlebotomist not have complete control over?

A) Specimen labeling
B) Patient preparation
C) Specimen collection
D) Collection equipment

43

Which of the following refers to a failure to give reasonable care by the health-care provider?

A) Negligence
B) Adverse event
C) Treatment incident
D) Medical malpractice

44

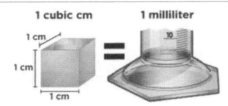

1 cubic cm = 1 milliliter

A **cubic centimeter** or "cc" is a commonly used liquid measurement in the medical field. It replaces "mL" in some of the instruments used for collecting specimens and applying medication.

Which of the following is the approximate equivalent of 10 ccs?

A) 3 mL
B) 5 mL
C) 8 mL
D) 10 mL

45

Which part of a patient should blood never be collected from?

A) The arm containing an IV
B) The arm containing a CVC
C) The arm containing an AV shunt
D) The arm containing an arterial line

46

The laboratory and clinical tests are performed under specific standards. These standards have been developed, improved, and studied for the benefit of the field.

Which of the following national organization develops guidelines and sets standards for laboratory procedures?

A) CAP
B) CLSI
C) CLIAC
D) NAACLS

## 47

The difference between **inpatient and outpatient care** is how long a patient must remain in the facility to have the procedure done. The advent of outpatient clinics ensures that patients are admitted to a hospital when they are seriously ill or have severe physical trauma.

Which of the following about inpatient care is true?

A) Inpatient care requires overnight hospitalization.

B) Surgeries, childbirth, and rehabilitation services are some examples of inpatient care.

C) Patients receiving inpatient care remain under the supervision of a nurse or doctor, and many types of professionals may assist them.

D) All of the above

## 48

Pneumatic tube systems (PTS) are necessary inventory in hospitals. These tube systems propel cylindrical containers through networks of tubes by compressed air or by partial vacuum.

Which of the following is true about the transportation of samples in PTS?

A) Samples must be enclosed in leak-proof material.

B) Gloves should be worn when removing samples from the container.

C) Samples collected by invasive procedures must be transported by hand and not delivered to the laboratory via the PTS.

D) All of the above.

49

In some hospitals, samples are transported to the laboratory through a PTS (pneumatic tube system).

Which of the following is right about the transportation of samples by PTS?

A) Samples must be appropriately cushioned to prevent breakage or red blood cell (RBC) hemolysis.

B) Delivery of samples through a PTS is a very efficient method because both personnel and delivery time are saved.

C) Pneumatic tube systems provide rapid transport of patient blood samples, but the physical stress of PTS transport can damage blood cells and alter test results.

D) All of the above.

50

Which of the following pressure reading should the blood pressure cuff remain during a bleeding time test?

A) 20 mm Hg

B) 10 mm Hg

C) 50 mm Hg

D) 40 mm Hg

51

Which of the following about phlebotomy is not correct?

A) Phlebotomists are the only health care personnel allowed to collect blood specimens.

B) Entry into phlebotomy programs usually requires a high school diploma or its equivalent.

C) Usually, a postsecondary nondegree award from a phlebotomy program is required to enter the occupation.

D) Phlebotomy technicians are usually supervised by a medical professional such as a clinical laboratory technologist.

52

The work of each healthcare department naturally specializes in a different part of the body. To understand general medical records, each of these body parts is vital.

Which of the following about the body parts is not correct?

A) Nasal means "Nose."

B) Ventral means "Stomach."

C) Pectoral means "Breast."

D) Digital means "Fingers and toes."

53

The digestive system acts as the food processor of the human body. The food is turned into energy that can be stored or used by the body.

Which of the following is an accessory organ of the digestive system?

A) Heart
B) Liver
C) Lungs
D) Bile duct

55

The **Clinical Laboratory Improvement Amendment (CLIA)** is a federal organization founded to regulate all clinical laboratory procedures in the country.

Which of the following laboratory professionals is specified by CLIA as responsible for administering a specific clinical area, such as chemistry?

A) Laboratory manager
B) Technical supervisor
C) Senior medical analyst
D) Medical technologist apprentice

54

Healthcare personnel must understand the structure, finance, and functioning of the health care system to help patients obtain quality care.

Which of the following about the health care structure in the US is correct?

A) Public Health Service (PHS) delivers health care to the citizens of the United States.
B) Department of Health and Human Services (HHS) protects and improves the nation's physical and mental health.
C) Inpatient (nonambulatory) and outpatient (ambulatory) support all three healthcare levels currently offered in the United States.
D) All of the above

56

How frequently is blood wicked during a bleeding time test?

A) Every ten seconds
B) Every five seconds
C) Every thirty seconds
D) Every forty-five seconds

57

Sputum is mucus collected from the trachea, bronchi, and lungs. Sputum samples are potentially infectious for active tuberculosis, and they must be immediately delivered to the laboratory and kept at room temperature before processing.

Which of the following is true about the Sputum samples?

A) The sample is obtained by deep coughing to bring sputum up from the lungs.
B) Samples should be collected from patients who have abstained from eating and drinking.
C) Before collecting the sample, the patient must be asked to rinse his or her mouth with water.
D) All of the above.

58

An outpatient visits a laboratory outside the hospital. He is asking for his blood to be drawn for a test.

Which of the following can be the reason for a phlebotomist to refuse this request?

A) Lack of health insurance
B) First-time for blood drawing
C) Failed to eat breakfast and is dizzy
D) Underage according to the state laws

59

The term "**hyperglycemia**" is derived from the Greek hyper (high) + glykys (sweet) + haima (blood).

Which of the following characteristics is observed when a person has hyperglycemia?

A) Low glucose levels
B) High glucose levels
C) Increased hemoglobin
D) Decreased hemoglobin

60

Lab result shows a range of numbers that serve as a reference to describe abnormality and normality on a disease tested to a patient.

Which of the following is needed before releasing any lab results of a patient?

A) Affidavit
B) Digital signature
C) Written permission
D) Call from physician

61

Medical terminology can contain a prefix, root word, a combining vowel, and a suffix to create medical terms. Medical terms describe medical aspects and diseases.

Which of the following medical term is not correctly defined or broken down into its parts?

A) Neuroblastoma is the disease of the nerve cells, and it is broken down as neuro-blast-oma
B) Myocarditis is an inflammation of the heart muscle, and it is broken down as myo-card-itis
C) Hyperthyroidism is the condition of overactive thyroid activity, and it is broken down as hyper-thyroid-ism
D) Gastroenterology is the branch of medicine focused on the digestive system and its disorders, and it is broken down as gastr-o-enter-o-logy.

62

Which of the following must be done in the case of an accidental needlestick?

A) Quickly wash the area with an antibacterial soap.
B) Express blood from the wound.
C) Contact your supervisor and report exposure.
D) All of the above.

63

Which of the following refers to misconduct by a health-care professional that results in injury to the patient?

A) Omission
B) Sentinel event
C) Chain of custody
D) Medical malpractice

64

It is crucial to understand the organizational structure of a Hospital for a healthcare worker because it makes the chain of command clear and facilitates the understanding of the hospital's functioning.

Which of the following is generally patients' first contact with a hospital?

A) Nursing
B) Admissions
C) Administration
D) Information services

65

The official "Do Not Use" list of the Joint Commission applies to all medication-related documents.

Which of the following is stated in The Joint Commission "Do Not Use" list?

A) Write "Unit" instead of "U"
B) Write "International Unit" instead of "IU"
C) Write "morphine sulfate" instead of "MS"
D) All of the above

66

Hospitals have an organizational structure that allows for the efficient management of departments. Healthcare workers must know how healthcare organizations operate.

Which of the following are among the responsibilities of administrative services?

A) Performing public relation duties
B) Overseeing budgeting and finance
C) Managing the operation of departments
D) All of the above

67

Medical institutes usually join a medical association for the sake of benefits. The institute will have to receive the acknowledgment of the association before they can join and meet the standard to be accepted.

Which of the following is the oldest and largest healthcare standards-setting body in the nation?

A) The Joint Commission
B) American Medical Association
C) College of American Pathologists
D) Center for Medicare and Medicaid

68

The main work of a phlebotomist is to collect blood from patients and test these samples to check for existing health issues, such as diseases, cholesterol, and bacteria.

Which of the following tasks is not considered as a phlebotomy competency?

A) Following all safety procedures
B) Handling a hematology blood analyzer
C) Utilizing the correct medical terminology
D) Choosing the right site for specimen collection

69

A phlebotomist must know the bottom line when acting for the sake of collecting samples from the patient. From a moral standard, it is okay to be rejected from time to time as long as it is impossible to acquire a specimen in a usual manner.

Which of the following is committed by a phlebotomist if he threatens a patient who refuses blood draw?

A) Assault
B) Adultery
C) Negligence
D) Defamation

CONTINUE ▶

70

People of different age groups usually have a group of specialized doctors who can take care of them.

Which of the following study deals with the problems that elderly individuals might encounter?

A) Pathology

B) Cardiology

C) Gerontology

D) Psychiatry

71

Which of the following sentences is the exact meaning of informed consent?

A) Patients waive their rights.

B) Patients must ask their doctors if they can have blood drawn.

C) The phlebotomist may draw a patient's blood without the patient's permission.

D) Patients must be informed of recommended treatments and their risks before they are performed.

72

Should I?

Ethics can be a questionable topic depending on the field you are working on. A country can recognize the behavior as ethical but, at the same time, unlawful in some cases.

Which of the following is a good definition of ethics?

A) Standard of care

B) Legally required conduct

C) Patient's preferred standard

D) Standards of right and wrong

73

All **specimens** must be labeled in the presence of the patient immediately after collection.

Which of the following is right about labeling a patient's specimen?

A) A phlebotomist must never pre-label specimen containers.

B) Incomplete or inaccurate labeling may result in the rejection of the specimen by the laboratory.

C) The patient's first name and last name, birth date, hospital medical record number, and collector's ID must be included in the label.

D) All of the above

74

Body cavities are the hollow spaces containing the internal organs.

Which of the following is true about the body cavities?

A) The dorsal cavity contains the cranial cavity and spinal cavity.

B) The abdominopelvic cavity combines the abdominal and pelvic cavities.

C) The ventral cavity consists of the thoracic cavity, abdominal cavity, and pelvic cavity.

D) All of the above.

75

Which of the following is a safe work practice for a phlebotomist?

A) Needles should never be recapped, removed, broken, or bent after the phlebotomy procedure.

B) All items used for the procedure must be disposed of according to the waste disposal policy.

C) In the case of an accidental needlestick, quickly wash the area with antibacterial soap, express blood from the wound, contact your supervisor and report exposure.

D) All of the above.

76

The patient must be identified upon being admitted to a hospital. The patient's information must be complete as much as possible and made private from the public's gossip.

Which of the following refers to proper patient identification?

A) Actively involving patients in their identification.

B) Asking a second person to verify your ID procedure

C) Scanning patient ID bands with barcode readers only

D) Checking the requisition against the patient's room number

77

Which organ is involved when a person has an inflammation of liver tissue or hepatitis caused by a virus or excessive alcohol use?

A) Heart

B) Liver

C) Brain

D) Ovaries

78

Which of the following is the abbreviation for microgram?

A) ml

B) mg

C) mm

D) mcg

80

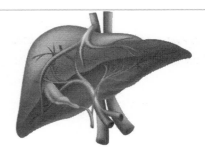

Which of the following is not a laboratory test that would help in the assessment for liver problems?

A) AST

B) GGT

C) ALP

D) ESR

79

Informed consent is a process to get permission before conducting a healthcare intervention on a person.

Which of the following is correct about informed consent?

A) Patients must have the legal and clinical capacity to give informed consent.

B) Informed consent requires the healthcare worker to thoroughly explain the procedure.

C) Healthcare workers must make sure that the patient understands and gives consent to every procedure.

D) When a doctor orders a blood draw or injection, the patient does not have the right to refuse any venipuncture, so the healthcare worker does not need informed consent.

81

Phlebotomists provide instructions and containers to patients for the collection of random samples.

Which of the following is true about the collection of samples?

A) Sweat electrolytes are collected for the diagnosis of cystic fibrosis.

B) Semen samples are collected for fertility studies and the effectiveness of a vasectomy.

C) Throat cultures are collected to diagnose the cause of an acute respiratory infection.

D) All of the above.

CONTINUE ▶

## 82

Monitoring a patient's health requires attention to detail and a keen eye for observing changes in the patient's situation. Detailed tests are also indicators of the health of the patient.

Which of the following are set up to monitor all areas of care that tend to cause problems?

A) Sentinel events
B) Threshold values
C) Quality indicators
D) Internal report forms

Aliquot means to divide specimens into smaller portions in separate tubes

Venous access is any method used to access the bloodstream through the veins.

A diluent is a solution (such as water or saline) that reduces a specimen's concentration.

Hypoxemia, low blood oxygen levels, is a sign of a problem related to breathing or circulation.

Warmed Specimens such as semen must be kept close to body temp, transported back to lab within 2 hours, and protected from bright light.

How many of the terms given above are defined correctly?

A) 2
B) 3
C) 4
D) 5

84

Which of the following terms is described as the inflammation of the vein walls?

A) Arthritis
B) Glossitis
C) Phlebitis
D) Pyelonephritis

85

Which of the following terms refers to the swelling of the body tissues, generally the tissues in the legs and arms, caused by excess fluids?

A) Edema
B) Eczema
C) Blastema
D) Erythema

86

From the time of Hippocrates, blood is being drawn from the patients.

Which of the following is correct about blood collection?

A) Patients have the right to refuse blood collection.
B) Patient consent must be taken before starting blood collection.
C) If a patient refuses blood collection, the phlebotomist should contact the patient's health-care provider and document the incident.
D) All of the above

87

Which of the following about the history of inpatient care is true?

A) The history of inpatient care goes back to 230 BC in India.
B) The first building for inpatient care was built by the Romans in 291 AD.
C) Florence Nightingale was the most famous inpatient care provider and the pioneer for improving medical care in the mid-19th century.
D) All of the above

88

The collection area is cleansed with a 70% alcohol-based solution. In specific laboratory tests, an iodine-based solution is used to prevent microorganisms from contaminating the blood sample.

In which of the following tests should alcohol wipes not be used when drawing samples?

A) ETOH level

B) Complete blood count

C) ETOH level and Blood cultures

D) ETOH level, Blood cultures, and Complete blood count

89

A **confirming response** acknowledges the understanding of a person to another person to value him/herself more.

Which of the following suggests a confirming response that a healthcare professional can give to a patient?

A) "I don't think we can give you that."

B) "I have no idea how long it will take."

C) "I understand how you must be feeling."

D) "I will just get back to you when I have done my schedule today."

90

What does the prefix derm- usually refer to?

A) Skin

B) Bone

C) Death

D) Blood

## 91

Lancet is a small pointed blade usually with two edges used for incising or puncturing.

Lumen is the hollow core of the vein, the best place for needle position during venipuncture.

T syringe is an instrument used to inject fluids into or aspirate fluids from any vessel or cavity.

Respirator is a device designed to protect the wearer from inhaling hazardous atmospheres.

Centrifuge is a device that spins laboratory specimens at high speeds to separate the samples into their components for testing purposes.

Defibrillator is a device that delivers an electrical shock to restore a normal heartbeat, to prevent or correct an arrhythmia, or to restore the heart's beating if the heart suddenly stops.

Some medical devices and instruments are defined above. How many of the definitions are correct?

A) 3
B) 4
C) 5
D) 6

## 92

Rules and regulations are usually created to set a standard for underemployed people.

Which of the following are principles of right and wrong conduct as they apply to professional problems?

A) Rules
B) Ethics
C) Kinesics
D) Guidelines

Patients have the right to sue phlebotomists and other medical professionals due to medical malpractice and negligence in the blood draw results.

Which of the following situations can protect a phlebotomist from a lawsuit?

A) Disregarding the patient's refusal to blood collection

B) Carrying out the employer's venipuncture procedures

C) Informing another person about the laboratory tests ordered

D) Utilizing the same blood collection processes on patients of all ages

The **transverse plane,** or horizontal (axial) plane, is an imaginary plane used to divide the body into superior and inferior parts. The coronal and sagittal plane is perpendicular to it.

Which of the following is the division caused by the transverse plane?

A) Vertically into right and left portions

B) Vertically into front and back portions

C) Diagonally into upper and lower portions

D) Horizontally into upper and lower portions

CONTINUE ▶

A patient can be complicated by refusing to cooperate with the healthcare professional. This type of patient will require more patience and skill to persuade.

Which of the following is the best way to handle this type of patient?

A) Refuse to collect a specimen from him or her.

B) Threaten to report this case to the authorities.

C) Help the patient to feel in control of the situation.

D) Let the patient know that refusing further will be a futile struggle.

Health–care–acquired infection (HAI) is a new term referring to an infection acquired by a patient due to a healthcare procedure.

HAIs also referred to as **Nosocomial Infections**, are used to designate an infection acquired by a patient during a hospital stay.

Which of the following is the reason for HAIs?

A) Contaminated air conditioning systems

B) Congested hospitals; beds close to one other

C) Personnel not following infection control practices; improper sterilization and disinfection practices

D) All of the above

## 97

Routine hematology includes the general analysis and diagnosis of blood samples. The results of the tests help the physicians determine the possible cause of the disease of the patient.

Which of the following is the abbreviation for the routine hematology test that includes hemoglobin, hematocrit, red and white blood count determinations?

A) CBC
B) PTT
C) CPK
D) CRP

Hospitals are the place for medication as well as hope. The church or the clergy usually visits the hospitals to pray for the patient's well-being and health.

Which of the following should you do if clergy is with the patient when you arrive to collect the specimens?

A) Return after the clergy left.
B) Ask the nurse to drive the clergy away.
C) Write the "Unable to collect specimen" remark.
D) Ask the clergy to pause first for you to collect specimen.

## 99

Which of the following sentences describes the characteristic of blood vessels known as arteries?

A) Arteries carry blood toward the heart.
B) Arteries have valves along the lumen.
C) Arteries have a thick muscle layer that lines the lumen.
D) Arteries are composed of a single layer of endothelial cells.

CONTINUE ▶

100

Edema is a collection of fluid under the skin.

The basal state is the state of rest and fasting, generally for at least 12 hours.

Sclerosis is the hardening, especially from inflammation and certain disease states.

Petechiae are the small hemorrhagic spots that appear under the surface of the skin.

Anemia is the condition of having less than the average number of red blood cells or hemoglobin in the blood.

Some medical conditions are defined above. How many of the definitions are correct?

A) 2

B) 3

C) 4

D) 5

101

In some medicines, the intake is measured by cup, teaspoon, or spoonfuls. All of these measurements have their "mL" equivalent with a small margin of error.

Which of the following is the approximate liquid measurement of one teaspoon?

A) 1 mL

B) 3 mL

C) 5 mL

D) 6.5 mL

102

Which of the following is not a personal characteristic that is required of a professional phlebotomist?

A) Honesty

B) Compassion

C) Dependability

D) Sense of humor

103

The **National Patient Safety Goals (NPSGs)** is a national standard accepted nationwide in healthcare institutes. It aims to protect the patient during every step of the healthcare process.

Which of the following establishes NPSGs ?

A) CLSI's standards and guidelines

B) TJC's annual safety requirement goals

C) Safety rules set down by CDC and OSHA

D) NAACLS national educational guidelines

## 104

Which of the following medical science is not defined correctly?

A) Microbiology is the study of microscopic organisms.

B) Rheumatology is the study of treating an illness by using radiation.

C) Pharmacology is the study of medicines and drugs used in medical treatment.

D) Immunology is the study of the body's resistance to disease and defense to foreign substances.

The blood vessels in the human body are interconnected. They are usually interlinked, depending on their sizes.

Which of the following are the longest vein and the largest artery in the body in that order?

A) Cephalic and femoral

B) Pulmonary and femoral

C) Great saphenous and aorta

D) Inferior vena cava and brachial

## 106

CSF (Cerebrospinal fluid) surrounds the brain and spinal cord, supplies nutrients to the nervous tissue, removes metabolic wastes and protects the brain and spinal cord against trauma.

Which of the following is true about the sample collection of CSF?

A) CSF samples should be handled with extreme care and delivered to the laboratory immediately.

B) Cerebrospinal fluid is collected to diagnose meningitis, subdural hemorrhage, and other neurological disorders.

C) Samples that are collected in sterile tubes are usually numbered 1 through 3. Tube 1 represents chemistry, Tube 2 represents microbiology, and Tube 3 represents hematology.

D) All of the above.

## 107

Balancing tubes equally in the rotor head and closing the centrifuge cover are the first safety rules for the centrifuge.

Which of the following is among the rules for centrifuge safety?

A) Do not recentrifuge samples.

B) Observe for excessive vibration.

C) Immediately stop and unplug the centrifuge when a tube is broken.

D) All of the above.

CONTINUE ▶

108

The medical practice of drawing blood from patients and taking the blood specimens to the laboratory for testing is called **phlebotomy**.

Which of the following is not included in phlebotomy skills?

A) Organization

B) Interpersonal skills

C) Being able to handle stress

D) Handling patient correspondence

109

Which of the following is the basic structural and functional unit of the kidney that regulates the concentration of soluble substances and water by filtering the blood, reabsorbing what is needed, and excreting what is not?

A) Neuron

B) Medulla

C) Thalamus

D) Nephron

110

Hemoglobin is the iron-containing protein that is responsible for the transport of oxygen in blood throughout the body.

Which of the following cellular components is responsible for the transport of hemoglobin?

A) Plasma

B) Electrolytes

C) Red blood cells (RBCs)

D) White blood cells (WBCs)

111

Thrombocytes, commonly known as platelets, are components of blood responsible for the clumping and clotting of blood vessel injuries to stop bleeding.

How long do platelets remain in circulation?

A) 2 to 5 days

B) 9 to 12 days

C) 10 to 20 days

D) One month

A measure of acidity or alkalinity of water-soluble substances pH stands for "potential of Hydrogen," and it is measured by pH meter. The allowable value of pH is from 1 to 14, with 7 as the neutral point. Values below 7 indicate acidity, and values over 7 indicate basicity.

What is the normal pH of blood in the body?

A) 3.80

B) 4.00

C) 7.35

D) 7.85

SECTION 7 BASICS OF PHLEBOTOMY

#	Answer	Topic	Subtopic	#	Answer	Topic	Subtopic	#	Answer	Topic	Subtopic	#	Answer	Topic	Subtopic
1	C	TA	S3	29	C	TA	S2	57	D	TA	S3	85	A	TA	S4
2	D	TA	S3	30	C	TA	S1	58	D	TA	S5	86	D	TA	S1
3	D	TA	S5	31	A	TA	S4	59	B	TA	S3	87	D	TA	S3
4	D	TA	S5	32	A	TA	S3	60	C	TA	S5	88	C	TA	S3
5	D	TA	S5	33	B	TA	S5	61	A	TA	S4	89	C	TA	S5
6	D	TA	S5	34	D	TA	S3	62	D	TA	S3	90	A	TA	S4
7	C	TA	S4	35	C	TA	S5	63	D	TA	S1	91	D	TA	S3
8	B	TA	S2	36	D	TA	S1	64	B	TA	S1	92	B	TA	S5
9	C	TA	S5	37	A	TA	S2	65	D	TA	S4	93	B	TA	S5
10	B	TA	S4	38	D	TA	S2	66	D	TA	S1	94	D	TA	S2
11	D	TA	S5	39	C	TA	S2	67	A	TA	S5	95	C	TA	S5
12	C	TA	S2	40	A	TA	S4	68	B	TA	S3	96	D	TA	S1
13	C	TA	S5	41	C	TA	S4	69	A	TA	S5	97	A	TA	S5
14	D	TA	S5	42	B	TA	S2	70	C	TA	S5	98	A	TA	S5
15	A	TA	S5	43	A	TA	S1	71	D	TA	S2	99	C	TA	S2
16	B	TA	S1	44	D	TA	S4	72	D	TA	S5	100	D	TA	S3
17	A	TA	S4	45	C	TA	S3	73	D	TA	S1	101	C	TA	S4
18	D	TA	S5	46	B	TA	S5	74	D	TA	S2	102	D	TA	S2
19	D	TA	S1	47	D	TA	S1	75	D	TA	S3	103	B	TA	S5
20	A	TA	S4	48	D	TA	S3	76	A	TA	S5	104	B	TA	S1
21	D	TA	S3	49	D	TA	S1	77	B	TA	S2	105	C	TA	S2
22	A	TA	S4	50	D	TA	S4	78	D	TA	S4	106	D	TA	S3
23	D	TA	S5	51	A	TA	S3	79	D	TA	S1	107	D	TA	S3
24	B	TA	S4	52	C	TA	S4	80	D	TA	S2	108	D	TA	S2
25	D	TA	S2	53	B	TA	S2	81	D	TA	S3	109	D	TA	S2
26	A	TA	S1	54	D	TA	S1	82	C	TA	S5	110	C	TA	S2
27	D	TA	S2	55	B	TA	S5	83	D	TA	S3	111	B	TA	S2
28	B	TA	S4	56	C	TA	S4	84	C	TA	S4	112	C	TA	S2

Topics & Subtopics

Code	Description	Code	Description
SA1	Health Care Structure	SA4	Medical Terminology
SA2	Human Anatomy & Physiology	SA5	Legal & Ethics
SA3	Introduction to Phlebotomy	TA	Basics of Phlebotomy

CONTINUE ▶

Made in the USA
Monee, IL
15 June 2024